CU00749779

"*Adventurous Learning* is a real gem for
Purposefully designing elements of uncer
educational experience may seem counter-intuitive, but as Simon
Beames and Mike Brown argue, these elements are essential to the
engaged and transformative 21st-century school and classroom. This
thought-provoking, useful book captures a critical and overlooked
element of educational design."
— **Jay Roberts**, *Earlham College, USA*

"A powerful book that speaks across outdoor and adventure education
and mainstream schooling. Simon Beames and Mike Brown cogently
argue for pedagogies for diverse purposes and contexts in order to
meet the challenge of rapidly changing societal needs. Their four
dimensions of adventurous learning—agency, authenticity, uncertainty
and mastery—are drawn from respected educational, psychological
and sociological theories and cohere into a readily understandable
framework. This will help teachers in any context to be clearer about
some important elements of teaching and learning in exciting and
engaging ways."
— **Sue Waite**, *Plymouth Institute of Education, UK*

"This elegantly written and deeply insightful book poses a revitalizing
adventure agenda for inside the classroom and out. In times when education for neoliberal replication is the norm, *Adventurous Learning*
embraces education for change, challenges entrenched ways of
learning and refocuses on the passions and agency of the learner."
— **Mike Boyes**, *MNZM, Associate Professor of
Outdoor Education, University of Otago, New Zealand*

"With the bankruptcy of conventional thinking about adventure
education becoming increasingly apparent, its advocates need to
reconstruct new foundations in an ever-more complex social,
intellectual and educational environment. Beames and Brown tackle
this challenge head on. By situating *adventure* in the context of
globalization and complexity, they decouple the concept from its
conventional association with the discourses of personal growth and
describe it instead as a potent arrow in the quiver to be used against
the forces that maintain factory-model schooling. The authors urge
teachers everywhere to make *all* learning adventurous—not by

encouraging physical risk-taking in faraway places or planning yet another trip to the teambuilding center, but by authentically partnering with youth to face the uncertainty that comes from addressing real challenges in their local communities—including the use of 'traditional' outdoor activities. If ever there was a book on adventure education deserving of a claim to John Dewey's legacy, this is it."

—**Jayson Seaman**, *University of New Hampshire, USA*

Adventurous Learning

Adventurous Learning interrogates the word 'adventure' and explores how elements of authenticity, agency, uncertainty and mastery can be incorporated into educational practices. It outlines key elements for a pedagogy of adventurous learning and provides guidelines grounded in accessible theory. Educators can adapt and tailor these guidelines for indoor and outdoor teaching in their own contexts. By reclaiming adventure and its role in learning, educators will be able to design and implement programmes based on sound principles that have deep and enduring meaning for their students in an increasingly complex, unpredictable and rapidly changing world.

Simon Beames is a senior lecturer in Outdoor Learning at the University of Edinburgh, Scotland.

Mike Brown is a senior lecturer in the Department of Sport and Leisure Studies, The University of Waikato, New Zealand.

Adventurous Learning

A Pedagogy for a Changing World

Simon Beames and Mike Brown

Routledge
Taylor & Francis Group

NEW YORK AND LONDON

First published 2016
by Routledge
711 Third Avenue, New York, NY 10017

and by Routledge
2 Park Square, Milton Park, Abingdon, Oxon, OX14 4RN

Routledge is an imprint of the Taylor & Francis Group, an informa business

© 2016 Taylor & Francis

Library of Congress Cataloging in Publication Data
A catalog record for this book has been requested

ISBN: 978-1-138-83165-0 (hbk)
ISBN: 978-1-138-83166-7 (pbk)
ISBN: 978-1-315-73648-8 (ebk)

Typeset in Berling and Bell Gothic
by Florence Production Ltd, Stoodleigh, Devon, UK

Contents

Foreword

Not more than a fortnight after news that *Adventurous Learning* was on its way to press, I received an email from a 14-year-old boy that, in the fullness of time, confirmed both the need for, and the wisdom contained within, this slim semi-revolutionary volume. And therein lies a story.

In his note, the boy explained that his Grade 8 teacher had asked all of the students in her two language arts classes in an elementary school in southwestern Ontario, Canada to read a book, any book, and to respond to it by writing a letter to its author. The book he had chosen was one called *Deep Waters: Courage, Character and the Lake Temiskaming Canoeing Disaster*—a book that I had written and published in 1996—that had been sitting around the house since he was born.

The reason it was in their house, he went on, was that his dad was in the book. His dad was one of the survivors of the St. John's School canoeing tragedy on Lake Temiskaming. His dad's older brother, an uncle he had never met, was on the trip too, but he had died. And that in spite of the fact that the fateful journey took place in 1978, the boy told me that the story was still "too new" for his dad to consider reading it. Encouraged by this assignment from his language arts teacher, the lad decided to read it for himself.

By that point in the note, it dawned that something quite remarkable was unfolding here: a 14-year-old boy reading a difficult story about his dad, when *he* was 14 and involved in a tragedy in which 12 teenage boys and one master died on a school canoe trip. The boy had questions about the details of the book, and about decisions I had made as a writer. But, as I began to ponder what I might say in response to his queries, these specifics were eclipsed by growing intrigue with the assignment itself.

In responding to their teacher's instruction, students made a rainbow of choices, from fiction to nonfiction, graphic novels, how-to books and everything in between. They all read their books during private reading time in their language arts classes and then, as part of the exercise, they all wrote letters to their authors, working through several drafts that were critiqued by peers and the teacher. Subsequently, students were put into groups and instructed to tell the others a little bit about their book and to read aloud their letter. For some students, this was as far as it went.

In an inspired next step for students who were particularly engaged, the teacher then gave anyone who was interested the time and opportunity to search out their author on the internet to see what else they had written, to see what else they might learn about them as writers and creators and, finally, to see if there might be a way to contact their author to send them the letter they had written.

Some of the authors were deceased, as it turned out, even though there was an abundance of material about them on the web. Other authors were local and writing for the first time and there wasn't much at all about them on the web. But for many of the students, they not only found evidence of their author online but they also found information— sometimes provided directly, other times through an agent or publisher— that looked like it might allow a letter to be sent. And that's how the connection was made between the son of the Lake Temiskaming disaster survivor and the author of *Deep Waters*.

I responded to the boy's questions, doing my best to answer with specifics, but I also told him how lucky he was to have a teacher who had created such an engaging assignment. Through his father's email address, we went back and forth a couple of times and this led to an invitation to attend the boy's class—basically for show-and-tell, to talk about what was turning into an epic learning experience for everyone involved. "You can talk about whatever you like," he said, "as long as my teacher says it's okay." And that's when things got even more interesting.

The more I contrasted this read-a-book-and-write-the-author assignment with what had happened with the goals of the school that had killed 12 boys and a teacher in the name of trying to "educate" them, the more I realized that there was an opportunity here to celebrate a sovereignly fine example of inspired classroom teaching. So I accepted the boy's invitation and turned up on the prescribed day at the agreed upon time.

By way of introduction, the boy told the class a bit about his book—my book—detailing his dad's experience at a school that was determined to "turn boys into men" by force feeding them Latin and Greek, by compelling them to clean the toilets, cook the food and commit great tracts of poetry to memory; by berating them or beating them with sticks when they misbehaved and, famously, by forcing them into insane snowshoe marches in the dead of winter and equally pointless canoe odysseys invoking the routes and virtues of the voyageurs—en route, or so they hoped, to building "character".

My job was to tell the class how far the teachers in *Deep Waters* had missed the educational mark by cajoling and dragging their students to the moral North Pole. I explained—and this was hard because the boy's father, who had lost his brother on the Temiskaming trip, as well as his mother and grandfather, were in the back of the room when our presentation was happening—how, through the misappropriation of pedagogical power, the Temiskaming school had permanently stained the educational invocation of risk. And, turning to the boy's teacher, I observed how much closer she had come to creating meaningful educational adventure by inviting students to participate in a language arts assignment that was, in my judgment, one of the most remarkable and enduring educational events I'd ever witnessed.

I talked about risk, about "learning edges" and how, in my estimation, you never learn anything when you're sitting in the fat, comfortable middle of what you know. Contrasting what the Temiskaming teachers were trying with their book assignment, I talked about the choices the language arts teacher had given them, including the various options and the risks—"I could have been a pedophile lurking on the internet," I told them—they took to seek out and connect with their authors. I talked about engagement and how this assignment, in this one instance, had allowed the boy to enter his father's world and, with the book and the assignment as a vehicle, to enter my world as well, and to meld the three in the most generative way by inviting me to his class.

The boy, as it turned out, was painfully shy but he had been captivated by the search for truth in the book he had chosen *and* in the detective-like and semi-clandestine hunt for the author. The assignment was situated within the rubric of the Grade 8 language arts curriculum but, because of the elements of choice with the book and in the shaping of the letter to the author and then in deciding whether or not to actually send the letter, the whole learning episode had relevance and intrinsic value for the students.

It was clear from the discussion with the class that followed our presentation that almost all the students in the class were thoroughly engaged, intrigued and energized by what they had done and, in this instance, by the serendipitous outcome of their assignment that had brought one author to the front of their class, and left a normally retiring and often invisible kid seriously chuffed at what he had done, beaming in the spotlight for a few moments on a sunny winter morning.

Adventurous Learning: A Pedagogy for a Changing World provides not only a worthy consideration of the social and theoretical context of this language arts assignment—bowing to Dewey and the likes of Festinger and Csikszentmihalyi, while bringing the conversation forward into Bauman's "liquid-modern" world as well—but also provides a lexicon of terms and a useful model for educators to employ as they seek to foster similarly powerful learning events in their own contexts. I have no doubt that teachers who are already disposed to this type of lesson construction will find resonance in these pages. As a reader and a member of the experiential education choir, I have found new meaning and relevance in visiting and revisiting the example of the language arts assignment through this book's generative quatrain lattice of authenticity, agency, uncertainty and mastery.

More significantly, however, I'm guessing that set in the disturbing context of 'McDonaldization' and 'Disneyization' of education, the arguments and guideposts herein—written in accessible, conversational and occasionally in charming self-effacing prose—will inspire teachers rooted in more conventional educational traditions to consider change, perhaps even to consider teaching as a political act. Practitioners working in more traditional outdoor adventure arenas, particularly those whose research broaches similar terrain, will also find the book stimulating, particularly the deliciously impertinent roasting-of-chestnuts-like metaphoric transfer of educational experience and challenge by choice. "If you teach anything," the authors boast early, "this book has something to say to you." Amen, Brothers Beames and Brown!

In a late 19th-century speech at Stanford University, railing against the post-industrial-revolution trends in education and calling for what he called "the moral equivalent of war", educational philosopher William James wrote: "Soft pedagogies have taken the place of the old steep rocky path to learning. But from this lukewarm air the bracing oxygen of effort is left out. It is nonsense to suppose that every step in education can be interesting. The fighting impulse must be appealed to. A victory scored under such circumstances becomes a turning point and crisis of character."[1]

This quotation has been something of a rallying cry for experiential educators intent on providing an alternative to conventional schooling. A hundred years later, Simon Beames and Mike Brown are pointing to an equally serious societal situation and calling for an equally impactful rethinking of education. But setting aside the fresh-air-fuelled notions of "steep rocky paths" to personal pedagogical enlightenment, and somewhat counter-intuitively, they have brought the revolution back into the classroom (without in any way discounting the potential power of the out of doors as a fertile learning ground) and, ironically, back into the lives and lifelong learning of students, back into the practice of educators with real potential to change the world.

James Raffan
Distinguished author, explorer and expedition educator
www.jamesraffan.ca

NOTE

1   *Talks to Teachers on Psychology: And to students on some of life's ideals* by William James. New York: Henry Holt and Company, 1899, pp. 54–55.

Preface

In the late winter of 2010, Simon led a group of ten university Outdoor Education students on a hut-to-hut ski tour in Norway. After six fantastic days of Nordic skiing in a gorgeous snowy landscape, with cosy evenings in fully provisioned huts complete with wood-burning stoves, we returned to our mountain lodge satisfied that our adventure had been a huge success.

The next morning, when we were due to take a bus and train to Oslo, and then a plane back to Edinburgh, we got the news that a volcano had erupted in Iceland and that all European air travel was cancelled. Our true adventure was just about to begin, and with it the seeds of this book.

Once in Oslo, we checked into the hostel that we had stayed in the previous week. In terms of group management, 'Maslow's' first level of needs had been met; our next task was to figure out a way to get home.

Perhaps the greatest difficulty in dealing with the situation was that the circumstances were very fluid and unstable. The airports, for example, did not know when flying would start again. It might be later today or it could be next week. I took a chance that afternoon and bought £1500 worth of air tickets for the next day. The group, split into two dorm rooms, was in good spirits. They Skyped family members and shopped for souvenirs.

We awoke the next day to disappointment and even greater uncertainty. Our 'new' flights would not materialize, as the airport was still closed, and the authorities had no idea when flights would begin again. This was getting serious.

We held a team meeting in the men's dorm room and got the issues on the table. The circumstances in which we found ourselves were constantly changing and could not be predicted, and the leaders (myself and Bob Henderson) had no prior experience of managing the obstacles ahead. We were all in this together and solving this puzzle would demand each individual's cooperation, ingenuity, selflessness and initiative.

Unlike the initial plans for our ski tour, I no longer held the upper hand in knowing the best mode of transport. In this situation, my knowledge acquired from previous trips was rendered useless. The solution to our dilemma would need to come from people in the group. Many ideas were floated: *we'll take the bus to Amsterdam and then a ferry to England*; *we'll rent a van and drive it back*; *we'll buy a second-hand van*; *we'll hire taxis to take us*; *we'll take a ferry to Copenhagen and then another to Newcastle*; and (my favourite), *we'll pay a fishing boat to take us across the North Sea*. By this time, it was late in the afternoon and we were weary after talking for hours. The next morning, however, a refreshed and determined group split into pairs and proceeded to gather information regarding the viability of each of the listed options.

When we gathered that afternoon, each pair reported back on the timing, cost and overall viability of the mode of travel they researched. Then we voted. The option deemed most viable was taking a two-day bus ride through Sweden, Denmark, and Germany, and finishing in The Netherlands. After staying the night at one of the student's parents' friend's apartments, we would take an overnight ferry to Harwich, on the east coast of England. Once there, we would be picked up by a student who would have driven a 15-seater minibus down from Edinburgh.

The next morning we embarked on a three-day odyssey. We arrived back in Edinburgh six days later than originally scheduled, and all of us felt that we had had an adventure.

In the weeks that followed, I tried to make sense of the events from that extended journey and was struck by a number of things. First, and perhaps most obviously, it seemed that getting back from Norway was much more adventurous than ski touring in Norway. If one was selling adventure in a glossy magazine, however, the ski touring would probably win every time. Second, I remember feeling that our ski tour had gone exactly how I had envisioned, but this feeling of the planned and predictable adventure did not sit well with me. What was it about the second part of our time away—figuring out how to get back from Oslo and then the travelling itself—that elicited such feelings of adventure? Did this adventure have fundamental ingredients?

Underlying our time in Oslo was an ever-present feeling of being in a 'fluid' situation. The possible courses of action were constantly shifting and no one possessed "definitive knowledge", such as when the planes would start to fly again. There was a high degree of *uncertainty*. What was certain was that we would eventually get back to Edinburgh—we just didn't know when or by what means.

Another feature that characterized our predicament was that it was real. The ski trip was ultimately a contrived set of experiences that I had packaged together because I thought they would be enjoyable and full of new learning experiences for my students. In contrast, part two of our Norwegian trip stood out because it was not contrived, nor planned in any way. It was a situation in which we found ourselves and from which no one could extract us. We couldn't turn this experience 'off' and then start again or do something different. We were fully immersed in a highly *authentic* set of circumstances. It was as real as it gets.

A third aspect of our trip was that the students had a large amount of power to decide how they were going to get themselves out of this situation. As a leader without any more information than the students, my task was reduced to that of facilitating healthy and productive discussions. Although the students obviously had nothing to do with choosing the challenge they faced, they had an enormous amount of *agency and autonomy*, in terms of proposing and evaluating different courses of action, choosing one, and then seeing it through.

Finally, this adventure demanded a high degree of psychological, socio-emotional and physical commitment from all of us. It did not involve negotiating hazards that might harm us, but it did present us with a variety of *challenges* that revealed themselves as time went on. These challenges demanded mastering skills in gathering and analysis, as well as deep reasoning regarding the outcomes associated with various courses of possible action. The challenges certainly required a certain mental and physical tenacity from all of us. Meeting these challenges demanded our best. I have never been so proud of a group that I've been away with.

Let's now fast-forward a couple of years to a time when Mike and I were at a conference, chatting about the problems of adventure education —how too many programmes have become overly predictable, commercialized and devoid of adventure. To us, it seemed that adventure education was going the same way as mainstream education.

Even though we both have backgrounds in outdoor adventure education, we work in Schools of Education at our respective universities. This affords us opportunities to spend time in schools and on outdoor programmes with school students. We were struck by how all kinds of education—indoor and outdoor, curricular and extra-curricular—was very prescriptive (i.e., with little uncertainty). Neither teachers nor students had strong voices regarding what was learned or how it was learned (i.e., little agency and autonomy). Further, much of the content was not taking place in the real world, where there are real problems to tackle: many of the forms of education that we witnessed had been relegated to classrooms and ropes courses (i.e., minimal authenticity). Finally, the vast array of learning activities on offer rarely demanded any depth of knowledge, skill, or judgment gained through experience and practice (i.e., minimal mastery).

We believe that learning through appropriate adventure is something that all teachers and instructors can facilitate—whether they are teaching nursery school, working at a summer camp or delivering a university geology lecture. This book aims to provide educators of all kinds with principles that will enable them to make their classes and courses more adventurous, in order for students to be more deeply engaged in learning that has a high degree of meaning and relevance to their lives.

SKB & MB

Acknowledgments

FROM MIKE . . .

I would like to thank Simon for his vision and for the enthusiasm that he brought to the project. Once again it has been a pleasure to work with you. My thanks to Juliet Small and Jane Townsend who provided valuable feedback on the manuscript at short notice. A special note of thanks to Nancy who put up with a 'lodger' during the final push to the finish on the book—your warm hospitality and friendship is greatly appreciated.

FROM SIMON . . .

I would like to thank John Telford, Beth Christie, Pete Higgins and Robbie Nicol for giving me time to read, think and write; Emily Salvesen and Fiona Reid, Pete and Mary Higgins and Hamish Ross, for giving me places in which to write; Naomi Silverman, at Routledge, for shepherding us so skilfully and genially through the publication process; Jennifer Broughton, Patrick Byrne, Scot Hoffman and Mitchell McLarnon, for providing incredibly helpful suggestions for improving the manuscript; James Raffan, for writing the Foreword; Mike, for his insightful thinking, humility and easy-going nature—all I need in a writing partnership; and Nancy, my ever supportive, tolerant and loving rock.

Chapter 1

Introduction

We are passionate about the role that well-conceived and facilitated educational experiences can play in enriching students' learning. Together we have over forty-five years of involvement in education, in a variety of roles, such as high school teacher, youth worker, outdoor instructor, university professor and researcher.

The rationale for this book is rooted in our concerns about the state of education in today's world and the path it is taking. We believe that the potential benefits of mainstream education and outdoor adventure education have been increasingly restricted and marginalized to a point where neither offers a strong platform for meaningful student learning. In this book we have articulated some of our concerns and made some suggestions for an alternative form of practice that we hope will both enrich students' learning experiences and stimulate educators who are seeking to broaden their repertoire of practice.

The state of any educational policy and practice is located within the greater social, cultural, political and economic times in which it exists. This may seem like an obvious statement, but it is an important one to begin with, as the content of this book would not have had so much relevance twenty or fifty or a hundred years ago. This book addresses a system of education that has been substantially shaped by a rapidly changing world that is a feature of the 21st century.

Consider how different life is now when compared to how it was for your parents or grandparents. Back then, there was no internet and there were no cell phones. Breathable fabrics and the use of plastic in the construction of kayaks were in their infancy. These new and improved material objects brought about by technological advances are easy to spot. The non-material aspects of 21st-century life are much harder to define, however. Many of these non-material aspects have affected social structures (e.g., notions of the family unit), career opportunities and lifestyle choices. Much of this has to do with (un)predictability and uncertainty regarding the future. These days, people are less likely to know what lies ahead of them, in terms of the jobs they will have, where they will live and how secure they might feel. Our lives are increasingly filled with uncertainty and speed. Giddens (1999) referred to this as the *Runaway World*.

Now consider two of the big criticisms that we hear about education in so-called 'developed' nations. You'll have heard that there is too much standardized testing and that classroom sizes are too big. These criticisms, which will be discussed in Chapter 3, are usually a consequence of educational budgets being under-supported by central or local/state governments, so that decisions about learning and teaching are often made on an economic basis, rather than on educational ones. In order to teach more people with fewer resources, an industrialized model of education, based on the rationalization of goods and services, is implemented.

Perhaps the most classic example of economic rationalization is what Ritzer (1993) labelled *McDonaldization*. With McDonaldization, organizations control, calculate and constrain their operations to such a degree that they become highly efficient. The positive side of this is that an organization's production can be highly predictable. This kind of prescribed operational process might be fantastic for an American traveller in Shanghai who wants to have a Big Mac; however, it is this standardization and prescription that is a major problem for contemporary education. One reason why this is a problem has to do with recognizing that people are not "all the same". When we treat everyone the same, we are making a judgment on what is best for people that is usually based on our understandings of what is good and right. What is valued in some societies as knowledge is ignored in others, and universalized 'knowledge' that is divorced from learners' historical and social contexts may be of little relevance or interest to them. The 'one size fits all' approach to education has failed a range of groups (e.g., indigenous peoples, immigrants and students from low socio-economic backgrounds).

We discussed earlier how education is a reflection of its time, and hopefully this idea is clearer now. The major challenges of our era, such as climate change, wars based on religious beliefs and public health (e.g., obesity, global pandemics), demand creative solutions that will not come from students who have learned to become excellent test-takers. Society needs young people who have been educated to address real-world issues on a planet that is moving swiftly.

It is through education itself that we have the means to change educational processes. Ken Robinson (2011) argues that we need to run our education systems in "radically different ways" (p. 5) if people are to survive and flourish. We are optimistic enough to believe that together we can provide some resistance to what might be termed 'the ills of education', but we are not so naive to think that this kind of change will happen overnight; it may take several years, if not a generation. Education is a highly politicized and complex enterprise with formalized learning outcomes, and educators have an ethical obligation to consider how the knowledge, skills and attitudes they teach are put to use.

This book has been written for a wide range of educators: early years teachers, primary school teachers, secondary school teachers, college and university professors, youth workers, wilderness expedition leaders, adventure activity instructors, corporate trainers and coaches. If you teach anything, this book has something to say to you. This may seem like a bold and even arrogant statement. Some may think that one book cannot possibly cater to such a wide audience. We believe that education of all kinds—indoor and outdoor, nearby and far away, with little people and big people—has gone down the same path to a point where there is less and less uncertainty (in terms of its outcomes and processes through which they are achieved), minimal participant power (what we call agency), fewer opportunities to learn in real-world, authentic settings, and too little emphasis is placed on mastering skills and knowledge that can be put to good use.

The book contains nine chapters that build on the foundations provided in this introductory chapter. In Chapters 2, 3 and 4 we outline some of the challenges and issues facing contemporary education, while in Chapters 5 to 8 we explain the four key dimensions of adventurous learning. We close the book with a chapter that discusses how the four dimensions can be considered together when designing and delivering engaging and meaningful learning for your students.

The forthcoming chapter delves into the meanings of adventure. As we will see, the definition of adventure is incredibly broad and one that many people will be able to make connections to in their home life, work, school and play. What do you think is an adventure? Consider the adventures that you have experienced in the last three months. Did these adventures happen by accident? Did you pay for these adventures? Did they involve 'typical' adventurous activities (e.g., paragliding, rock climbing) or did they involve something unexpected happening (e.g., getting a flat tyre while driving)?

In today's world, the word adventure means many things to many people; it is subjective and culturally relative. What constitutes an adventure for one of us may be utter boredom for someone else, and while our white, privileged male selves may seek adventure to construct and maintain a certain identity in society, people living in different circumstances (e.g., unemployment or social deprivation) may have no desire to augment the considerable levels of uncertainty and risk they involuntarily face on a daily basis.

Themes of adventure pervade western society and are evident in the choices people make about everything from clothes, to holidays, to leisure activities, from the dominant modes of charity fundraising, to children's birthday party activities, and even the post-apocalyptic video games that are so popular. What do these kinds of adventure have to do with education? Not very much, we would answer! We do argue, however, that meaningful education in the 21st century demands characteristics of adventure. There is an urgent need to reclaim the essence of 'adventure' and more deliberately incorporate key elements of it into our educational practices.

Chapter 3 is entitled the *Socio-cultural Backdrop*, and explores how our taken-for-granted, day-to-day actions are in fact highly influenced by the fast-paced, sophisticated and powerful economic forces that pervade society. One of the tensions present in contemporary society, which is in an increasing state of flux and uncertainty, is that many people crave predictability (perhaps as a consequence of this fluidity). Consequences of late modernity's rationalized features of social life manifest themselves through increasing regulation, standardization and prescription in both mainstream education and non-school-based outdoor education.

We will see how the collective theses within Beck's (1992) *Risk Society*, Giddens' (1991) *Modernity and Self-Identity*, and Bauman's (2007) *Liquid Times* give us a theoretical platform upon which we can examine what we mean by adventure. Notions of adventure, risk, challenge and uncertainty can only be considered within a micro (educational) context once they have been understood on a global, socio-cultural level. This discussion becomes more complex when we take the changing young person into account as well. The educational adventures that a 'digital native' child, who is largely disconnected from the natural world, might want to undertake, will contrast greatly with those of someone born even thirty years ago. Universalized and context-free adventure activities delivered to school students in many western countries fail to connect with the lived-experiences of youth in a globalized age.

For some people, the antidote to the pitfalls of conventional schooling could be found in organizations like Outward Bound, the National Outdoor Leadership School (NOLS) and Project Adventure. Over the last fifty years, however, outdoor adventure education, with its promise of personal and social development, has fallen into the same trap of rationalization, prescription and regulation as has mainstream schooling— the very style of education to which it was claiming to be an alternative. The 'naturalness' of highly orchestrated and contrived adventure pursuits being delivered by experts in 'place-ambivalent' settings, has been questioned by a number of writers. Formerly uncontested notions of the importance of perceived risk and the transfer of learning from one social situation to another are no longer philosophically supportable and are poorly evidenced. Adrenaline-filled fun activities invariably require so much knowledge and judgment for safe participation, that inexperienced young people are only able to exercise minimal agency and authentic decision-making.

The focus on delivering a bewildering array of activities alongside inescapable forces of commercialization (with their need for efficiency and predictability) has, paradoxically, eviscerated the potential for adventurous learning within contemporary adventure programmes. Chapter 4 provides a multi-faceted, coherent argument that outlines how outdoor adventure education, in its dominant guise around the world, fails to meet its full potential. Such a critique is a necessary platform upon which we can begin to redefine this critical relationship between adventure and learning.

At this point in the book, the scene has been set and we move to explaining how the four dimensions of adventure *(authenticity, agency, uncertainty and mastery)* can inform the development of an adventurous learning environment.

Chapter 5 on Authenticity explains how it is vitally important for students to see the value in the tasks in which they are engaged. This is not always the case, as educational activities are frequently viewed by students as a sequence of tasks to complete in order to succeed in some kind of assessment, which then permits progression to some kind of next stage, but which has few (if any) concrete, useful links to their daily lives. Our view of authenticity in education is rooted in what might be called 'real-world' learning contexts. Of course, classrooms are in the real world, but (at best) they are often one step removed from the democratic issues, cultural practices and curriculum-imbued surroundings that exist outside school buildings.

Our notion of authenticity is linked to Dewey's call for education not to be viewed as preparation for the future, but rather, be full of meaning in the present. Authentic experiences are those that have deep relevance with the current lives of our students, rather than the acquisition of abstract knowledge (or Freire's notion of 'banking') that may be useful in the future. Unlike decontextualized ropes courses and algebra exercises, authentic learning opportunities *here and now* help students to understand and learn from the world as experienced in the present. Many authentic learning contexts exist in the school grounds and local neighbourhood, while others involve working with community organizations in service, conservation, citizenship or enterprise projects.

For students to engage deeply in learning they need to be provided with opportunities for ownership and responsibility. Another word for having this kind of power—one adored by sociologists—is *agency*. Agency is the focus of Chapter 6. Young people have a hunger and curiosity to learn about the world they inhabit, and we advocate for students to be equipped with the skills, knowledge and power to be able to make informed decisions regarding the circumstances they encounter throughout their educational career.

This is not to vanquish the role of educators, as they are central to the quality of their students' education. Indeed, although we are perhaps stating the obvious, unlike learning—which people have been doing since the beginning of time in the absence of formal schooling—education involves an educator (Itin, 1999; Roberts, 2012). Educators' reason for being is to facilitate learning that will help students and society benefit in equal measure. In adventurous learning environments, their role (in our view) is to consider the value of sequenced learning experiences that afford students opportunities to evaluate various courses of action, construct and execute plans, and be prepared to deal with consequences. Agency is a crucial dimension in our conceptualization of adventure and is interwoven with our development of the concept of mastery through challenge.

The third dimension in adventurous learning is Uncertainty. This chapter outlines the vital necessity of pedagogical approaches that feature uncertainty of outcomes and of process. Our approach to adventurous learning contrasts with commercialized, packaged and highly regulated 'adventures' that feature replicable and predictable outcomes, and which are so typical of many tightly scripted contemporary adventure education programmes. School-based educators inhabit a world of set lesson plans with pre-determined outcomes and pressure to cram-in packaged content within a fixed time frame. A distinguishing feature of our conception of uncertainty is the emphasis placed on process and the need to create space for learners to exercise curiosity and creativity, rather than restricting these attributes through rigid adherence to defined lesson plans or achieving predetermined outcomes.

We are calling for a reappraisal of educational activities of all kinds, so that students can experiment, learn from trial and error, and make mistakes without the threat of physical or psychological harm. This is not wrapping our students in cotton wool; it is about providing space for experimentation within carefully considered boundaries. Indeed, powerful learning experiences can come about when neither the teacher nor the students know the solution to a given problem and must work together to find it. The rationalization of mainstream educational outcomes, coupled with the standardization and commercialization of adventure activities (that require replicability and certainty), undermine student agency and severely limit what can be learned and how it can be learned. Following Dewey's notion of the *indeterminate situation*, uncertainty is a cornerstone of adventurous learning.

Chapter 8 discusses the crucial ingredients of Mastery through challenge. We know that not enough challenge leads to boredom and too much often results in feelings of helplessness or inadequacy. We are concerned that adventure-based educators have been culpable of confusing discussions of educational challenge by using the terms 'risk' and 'challenge' almost interchangeably. This has led to the development of 'novel' activities that, while fun, take the form of entertainment rather than education, thus diminishing opportunities for learning.

Appropriate challenges requiring the acquisition and application of skills are vital to enduring learning and can contribute significantly to building one's positive sense of self, thus underscoring the role of agency in attaining goals. In our view, the mastery of skills has an important role to play in developing learners' capacity to act and to be responsible for their choices. Appropriate learner-driven challenges, with their ensuing struggles, frustrations and successes, can lead to high levels of satisfaction.

We are conscious of young people's needs for authentic challenges that have meaning in their everyday lives; 'real-world' challenges lie in opposition to contrived tasks, such as rappelling off a tower or crossing a 'toxic swamp' using three planks of wood, which some people may find challenging, but from which limited useful and applicable learning may result.

We do our students few favours when we mistake high thrills entertainment for learning; entertainment may lead to short-term pleasure, but meaningful, enduring learning requires sustained effort. Too often, short-term novel activities do not demand that participants take control of the direction of their learning through developing and applying skills that build on prior knowledge. While suitable challenges may involve elements of risk, we strongly argue that artificially constructed physical risk-taking has no place in our conception of adventurous learning. The discussion needs to be centred on suitable, authentic learner-based challenges that lead to learning, rather than on fabricated and highly regulated activities that bear little resemblance to the challenges faced in real life.

The final chapter is where we explain how the features of adventurous learning—authenticity, agency, uncertainty and mastery—come together to guide practice and programme development. We present a schematic representation of adventurous learning that can be used to evaluate current educational practice and to inform future programme design, lesson planning and approaches to teaching. We are understandably cautious about the provision of 'the model' of adventurous learning, but we are also aware that as practising educators it is helpful to be able to have a conceptual model upon which to frame one's day-to-day thinking about how best to prepare today's learners for a changing world.

SUMMARY

The purpose of this book is to examine ways in which aspects of adventure can enhance indoor and outdoor teaching practices and positively influence learners. For us, this examination is not possible without having a deep understanding of both the various meanings of the word 'adventure' and the context of education in the early 21st century. Our belief is that too many educational enterprises dressed as adventure education are not very adventurous at all and, because of this, the amount of learning that they are capable of eliciting is greatly limited. The book's discussion moves us towards an enriched pedagogical approach that will provide early years teachers, primary school teachers, secondary school teachers, pre-service teachers, college and university professors, youth workers, wilderness expedition leaders, adventure activity instructors, corporate trainers and coaches with the tools to critically reflect, evaluate and develop their practice.

We encourage you to engage with the material presented with a questioning frame of mind, to engage in dialogue with your peers, and to experiment with the ideas put forward. Like you, we grapple with the day-to-day practicalities of teaching and the associated administrivia that seems to be the 'lot' of educators in modern educational institutions. The ideas that follow are drawn from our own trial and error, frustrations and successes, and desire to better equip those with whom we interact to be better prepared for a world that will not decrease in complexity and uncertainty.

You'll notice that we use the term 'adventurous learning' throughout the book, as opposed to adventure education. The word 'adventurous' is particularly appealing to us, as it comes with less 'baggage' than the ubiquitous term 'adventure', which is discussed in Chapter 2. The *Oxford Concise Dictionary* (2008) defines adventurous as "Open to or involving new or daring methods or experiences" (p. 19). It follows, then, that the kind of learning that we espouse be hallmarked in this same way.

We shared an earlier draft of the book with colleagues who acted as critical friends and kindly suggested improvements and modifications. Some reviewers found it helpful to skip ahead to the final chapter and see how the four dimensions of adventurous learning could be illustrated with diagrams. Others wanted to get to the 'solutions' part of the book first (from Chapter 5 onwards) and come back later to the 'issues' section (Chapters 2–4). Both of these ways of approaching the book are perfectly acceptable; indeed, in a book on adventurous learning, we wouldn't want to be too prescriptive to our readers. You have our permission to move between chapters in whatever order you like.

With this introduction, we warmly welcome you to the uncertainty and challenge of adventurous learning. We hope you will gain the knowledge and desire to develop authentic learning experiences for your students and implement this approach in your own contexts.

Chapter 2

Meanings of Adventure

Dictionary definitions, although necessarily brief, can provide a useful entry point into a discussion about a particular concept or term. The *Oxford English Dictionary* (n.d.) defines an adventure as, "A course of action which invites risk; a perilous or audacious undertaking the outcome of which is unknown; a daring feat or exploit", while Wikipedia (n.d.) defines adventure as "an exciting or unusual experience. It may also be a bold, usually risky undertaking, with an uncertain outcome . . . fraught with physical, financial or psychological risk, such as a business venture, or other major life undertakings". These 'common sense' understandings are worth bearing in mind as we begin to examine the meanings of adventure.

In this chapter we will:

- Look at how the term adventure has been used in different contexts.
- Demonstrate ways that adventure has been appropriated to serve particular economic or social functions.
- Examine existing definitions of adventure.
- Provide some signposts that shape our thinking about what constitutes an adventure when we are interested in fostering learning.

HOW MIGHT WE DEFINE AN ADVENTURE?

Beames and Pike (2013) suggest that the meaning of adventure is contested and not easily defined, while Varley (2006) suggests that "its meaning is subjective and fluid" (p. 174). In one of the early influential books that promoted adventure in education settings, Colin Mortlock (1984) asserted that,

> To adventure in the natural environment is consciously to take up a challenge that will demand the best of our capabilities—physically, mentally and emotionally. It is a state of mind that will initially accept unpleasant feelings of fear, uncertainty and discomfort, and the need for luck, because we instinctively know that, if we are successful, these will be counterbalanced by opposite feelings of exhilaration and joy.
>
> (p. 19)

A central tenet of many definitions of adventure is that it contains a degree of uncertainty regarding the outcome (Higgins, 2001; Hopkins & Putnam, 1993; Mortlock, 1984; Priest, 1999). Priest viewed adventure as a subset of the leisure experience; thus the following criteria needed to be met for an experience to thought of as an adventure. First, an activity needs to be entered into voluntarily; second, it needs to be intrinsically motivating—that is you engage in an activity because it gives you a sense of pleasure or enjoyment; and finally, the outcome is not known in advance. Priest suggests that, "the outcome of an adventure is uncertain when information (critical to the completion of a task or the solution of a problem) is missing, vague, or unknown" (p. 112). Seen this way, if we freely choose to participate in an activity we find enjoyable, but we are not sure of the final outcome, it may be classified as an adventure.

Another key term associated with uncertainty is risk: if an outcome is uncertain, there is the risk that the participant might lose something of value. For example, the risk might be getting wet when learning to kayak, falling and spraining an ankle when bushwalking, or—to use a home example—wasting time, money and effort when a do-it-yourself plumbing job goes wrong. However, this is only one side of the 'risk equation'; there are many potential positives from embracing uncertainty. Examples include financial gain (entrepreneurs/innovators embrace uncertainty), the acquisition of new skills (learning how to ski or surf involves a degree of uncertainty) or gaining new social networks when you start university or a new job.

Here's a simple example that meets the criteria of an adventure as suggested by Priest (1999). Mike recently went on a three-day mountain bike trip in a remote area with a group of friends; it was in his holiday time, he enjoys biking and the camaraderie of small group travel and there was some uncertainty about how long the trip would take and whether

11

there would equipment failure. In contrast, a police officer who enters a darkened building in pursuit of an offender might face uncertainty, but given it is part of their employment and thus not freely chosen, we would not consider this to be an adventure.

So far these three criteria seem like a reasonable basis for determining what might constitute an adventure. They clearly have some merit and allow for simple categorization of an activity as either an adventure or not an adventure. Let's briefly return to the example of Mike's mountain biking trip. His intention when going on the trip was to have a fun time with old friends in beautiful scenery and to get some exercise. In his mind there was no sense of this being an adventure; it was recreational and the degree of uncertainty (taking a bit longer, breaking some gear or getting a few scratches) was accepted as a normal part of an outdoor recreation experience. He wasn't seeking an uncertain outcome and he clearly intended to be home after a few days—refreshed and with good memories. He's not an expert mountain biker, but he is competent and fit; he knew that he had the skills to ride the track. However, if he had taken his mother along, she might have found the whole experience quite daunting. She no longer has the fitness to ride for three consecutive days, nor the technical riding skills to ride a bike on a narrow steep track. So, for her, the trip may have been an adventure, or a misadventure, as the level of uncertainty of outcome and the relative demands on her were too high; those three days would have become an ordeal.

This example illustrates an important point about the meanings that individuals attach to experiences. As Beames and Pike (2013) note, "what one person deems adventurous may not be to another person" (p. 2). What we consider to be an adventure is relative to our experience and the context. In particular, it depends on what we consider to be an 'uncertain outcome' and on our appreciation of, and acceptance of, risk. Clearly, a multi-day mountain biking experience can be thought of as an adventure, but we'd guess that few of us would consider the transport to the start of the track as an adventure. Yet if we apply Priest's (1999) three criteria, driving a car can be justifiably be seen as an adventure, as it is freely chosen, often pleasurable, and—as road accident statistics prove—contains a relatively high degree of uncertainty of outcome.

If we take our point a step further, going shopping for a new pair of shoes can be an adventure. Shopping is a leisure activity and the outcome is uncertain (e.g., high heel or flat, closed toe or open toe, black or red). If you think for a few minutes, we're sure that you can come up with many examples of day-to-day activities that could now be classified as an adventure. We run the risk of many activities being thought of as an adventure and thus adventure being lost as a meaningful concept. Swarbrooke, Beard, Leckie and Pomfret (2003) attempt to capture the breadth and ambiguity of the meanings associated with the word 'adventure'. They highlight ten characteristics: uncertain outcomes, danger and risk, challenge, anticipated rewards, novelty, stimulation and excitement, escapism and separation, exploration and focus, and contrasting emotions. While not every one of these characteristics of adventure is helpful in our discussion of adventure and its relationship to learning—artificially elevated levels of danger and risk have no place in education—this list illustrates the multi-faceted connotations of the word.

While Priest's (1999) definition and Swarbrooke et al.'s characteristics together serve as a useful starting point, our discussion needs to delve a little deeper. What is clear is that the meanings that an individual brings to an activity, coupled with their previous experience and knowledge, have a profound influence on how they perceive what is an adventure experience.

What is also apparent from the literature is that it is not the activity itself that makes something an adventure. A good example of this is the rise of adventure tourism. Many tourists visit countries such as New Zealand or Norway to partake in adventure activities. For many of these people, sky-diving or white-water rafting might be both sold, and consumed, as adventures. For the tourist, being seen to be an 'adventurer', to wear the t-shirt, and to have the photo (and to post it on social media) signifies an aspect of their adventure identity. Yet for the adventure guide, be they a tandem sky-diving instructor or a rafting guide, this is another day at their place of work. And as with any workplace there will be some level of uncertainty (e.g., Will the elevator break down? Will I make that sale?). Admittedly, it is a different type of uncertainty, but the meaning that we give to it depends on the individual's and business's tolerance and understanding of uncertainty, and the likelihood and severity of losing something of value. The adventure tourism guide expects to go home at the end of the day and sees the act of jumping out of a plane or negotiating a rapid very differently from a tourist who is paying for an adventure experience. Varley (2006) explains that, from the professional guides' perspective, "creativity, chaos and freedom will be generally undesirable elements in the supply of commodified, risk-assessed experiences offered for paying customers" (p. 177).

The issue of adventure (in terms of uncertain outcomes and risk) in tourism activities has been the subject of several studies (see Fletcher,

13

2010; Holyfield, 1999; Holyfield, Jonas & Zajicek, 2005). These writers highlight the tension between providing 'safe' adventures that give the appearance of being risky and the desire of tourists who possess limited knowledge and skills, but who want an adventure without actually being at risk of being harmed. That is, after all, why they pay for a commercial service. The tourism operator who 'waters down' the perception of a real adventure might quickly lose clients who find the experience too tame, too inauthentic or too much like a theme-park ride. What is sold as an adventure by professional providers and is supported by slick marketing material may not contain much uncertainty at all. The 'trick', if you will, is to convince the consumer that real risk is involved, that their active involvement is required, and that they really are partaking in an adventure. Through skilful choreography and the use of appropriate props and rehearsed narratives, the perception of adventure becomes the reality for consumers (see, for example, Cater & Dash, 2013).

Adventure tourism, while not the focus of this textbook, provides us with some interesting questions regarding the role of the 'novice' participant: the consumer of an adventure activity. We suggest that the positioning of the consumer in adventure tourism is frequently mirrored in the positioning of the student in many adventure education settings. The tourist participating in a white-water rafting trip is required to follow instructions, therefore opportunities to develop skills or show initiative is limited by the operational constraints (time, policies and procedures, and the need to cater for all ability levels) required to run a tourist operation. While we might discuss notions of adventure in terms of uncertainty and risk, in reality a business will want to develop predictable and safe trips where the clients are largely shielded from foreseeable harm. This is not to deny that risks exist, but a tour operator will have developed management plans and strategies that corral participants into relatively predictable roles. In many ways, both staff and clients are actors playing out roles that enable certain courses of action, but which subtly limit deviations from the script. Wherever possible, 'uncertainty' and foreseeable risks are eliminated or mitigated. Products that are delivered on a commercial basis and which inevitably fall under the regulatory framework of government agencies also need to comply with relevant legislation.

It has been suggested that an undue emphasis on risk and uncertainty in adventure tourism is misplaced. Cater (2006) has shown that the prime motivation for participating in adventure activities is "thrill and excitement" (p. 321), rather than a desire to take a risk. This has led Cater to argue that theoretical models connecting the pursuit of risk as the motivating reason for participating in adventure activities are "fundamentally flawed" (p. 321). Rather, adventure tourism activities are really focused on the provision of "choreographed and comfortable fun" that comes from providing a rush, and not the risk (Buckley, 2012, p. 963).

Laing and Crouch (2009) propose that one of the reasons that people undertake adventurous travel is for a more authentic or 'real' experience than that provided in everyday life, while Walle (1997) has suggested that adventure tourists may be looking for knowledge and insight rather than risk. It has also been suggested that participating in adventures provides opportunities for people to explore new roles or different expressions of identity (Laing & Crouch, 2009). For example, participating in a multi-day backcountry horse trek might allow someone to play out the role of the rugged frontiersperson, which sits in contrast to their day-to-day life as an office manager.

The desire for authenticity, in being fully engrossed in meaningful actions, is one of the attractions of adventure activities. Whether this is referred to in terms of Csikszentmihalyi's (1990) concept of flow (discussed in greater detail in Chapter 8) or through Becker's (2003) quest for "experiencing pure authenticity" (p. 91), there is clearly a desire for people to engage in adventures beyond taking a risk just for the sake of it; in other words risk-taking is not the goal of adventure. Central to both Cater and Becker's conceptions of adventure is embodied engagement, where one is exposed to a gamut of emotions and possibilities for gaining something of value.

From this brief discussion of adventure, primarily based on the notion of uncertainty/risk, we can see that simple recourse to an element of uncertainty of outcome is problematic. Many things in life are uncertain, but they are not necessarily considered to be an adventure. Likewise, the skills and experience that individual participants bring to activity will alter the degree to which they view it as an adventure. Merely labelling an activity as an adventure (or in today's terms, 'extreme sport') is not helpful either. In order to develop a more nuanced, and ultimately more helpful, definition of adventure that might underpin productive teaching and learning strategies, it is helpful to briefly discuss how adventure has been increasingly positioned as an alternative to the 'dullness' of everyday western life (see, for example, Elias & Dunning, 1986). Viewed from this perspective, adventure is 'outside' everyday life, yet at the same time is heavily commodified and predictable: it has fallen under the rationalizing processes to which it seeks to be an alternative. The next section provides an initial foundation that we develop further in Chapters 3 and 4.

PARADOXICAL ASPECTS OF ADVENTURE

To gain a more nuanced perspective of adventure we now turn to a paper by Lynch and Moore (2004), who adopted a socio-historical approach as the basis for their analysis. One of the strengths of their paper is the extension of discussion beyond the realm of adventure as an individual preference or disposition (i.e., beyond merely psychological explanations). While they acknowledge that individuals may seek adventure to fulfil internal needs and desires, they contend that a richer understanding can be gained if we see adventure as "expressions of economic, political and cultural processes" (p. 9) that have been appropriated to serve a number of ideological ends. They argue that adventure "is a central pillar of modern capitalist discourse" (p. 6) and detail how it has underpinned private and state-sponsored economic expansionism, been used in the provision of recreation and leisure experiences and employed as a vehicle for personal development (e.g., therapeutic interventions, outdoor education and corporate training).

Lynch and Moore (2004) present two paradoxes that are inherent in adventure experiences. The first relates to the use by adventurers of advanced technical equipment and technology (e.g., emergency locator beacons, satellite phones, breathable fabrics). These "prosthetics" (p. 3) largely mitigate many of the risks associated with an adventure (see also Wurdinger & Potter, 1999). One only has to open an outdoor magazine to realize how predominant the advertisements for new equipment are, or view any one of a number of YouTube clips to see the ubiquitous sponsors' logos that are captured for marketing purposes.

The second paradox identified by Lynch and Moore "is the conflict between the use of adventure to provide experiences supposedly 'missing' in contemporary societies and the extensive centrality of notions and ideologies of adventure in the history, literature and process of economic expansion of these same societies" (p. 3). This paradox highlights the dominance of an adventure ideology that has underpinned the development of western industrialized societies, while simultaneously promoting adventure as an escape from that same world.

An example of this absurdity is how we are encouraged to take risks in the business world—to innovate, to be creative, and to rise to the challenges of a constantly changing marketplace. On the flip side, however, we are also encouraged to take an adventure holiday to escape from the stresses that our work-life causes. The idea that undertaking an adventure in a natural environment would counter-balance the corrupting influences of modern life can be traced to works of the Romantic poets and writers such as Wordsworth, Coleridge and Rousseau. These Romantic writers reiterated earlier versions of the 'adventure myth' that follow a fairly standard formula: a perilous journey, a struggle or battle, perhaps an encounter with monsters or ordeals of loneliness and hunger (Zweig, 1974; Farley, 2005; Loynes, 2010). This escape from the mundane life also features in the promotion of adventure in outdoor education textbooks such as Mortlock's (1984) *The Adventure Alternative*, where adventures are claimed to provide an escape from the "anxieties of modern existence" (p. 19). Lynch and Moore (2004) argue that a large body of literature regards adventure as "a psychological palliative against the ravages of everyday life in the later twentieth century" (p. 4).

As a slight aside, Varley (2006) has questioned whether the very term adventure "is in fact simply a product of the leisured imaginations of those who live in comfort and convenience-obsessed modern industrialised countries" (p. 192). Varley's point is pertinent as it raises questions about the cultural bias, or unexamined worldviews that we might hold. Adventure has meanings for particular groups of people in western cultures that may have little or no relevance to others in their own society, let alone other cultures. For example, it has been argued that adventure 'masks' ideological positions that reinforce male superiority and white-ness. In a thought-provoking article, Farley (2005) examined the rise of 'Shackletonmania' in the late 1990s and early 2000s. She explored the reasons why the polar explorer Ernest Shackleton regained popularity in the adventure tourism and business management consultancy arenas. She argued that Shackleton's position as an adventure hero, and his resurgence as a modernday cultural icon, was closely linked to ideas surrounding "hegemonic discourses of masculinity and whiteness . . . he embodied a model of manly white explorer integral to British imperialism" (p. 232). He represented particular ideals of masculinity: physical strength, self-sacrifice, resilience in face of adversity and a type of leadership that appeals to corporates. Shackleton's re-emergence after decades of neglect was contingent upon the intersection of various social, political and economic factors, rather than the inherent newsworthiness of his endeavours eighty years after the event.

It is clear that the links between adventure, capitalism and empire-building have a long tradition. Nerlich (1987) traces the development of merchant adventurers who funded voyages of discovery in the hopes of finding gold, spice or new territories. Lynch and Moore (2004) contend that the ideology of adventure continues to permeate contemporary western societies. For example, while the modern businessperson no longer has to embark on a literal journey of exploration, they can be an adventurer through their actions in economic enterprises and project an adventurous identity through appropriate recreational activities (see Foley, Frew & McGillivray, 2003). By extension, the discourses of adventure find fertile ground in educational contexts where young people are shaped to be producers and consumers in a global economy that has been created by previous generations.

This brief section has shown that the promotion of adventure as an alternative to 'everyday life'—whether it be commercial tourism or outdoor education experiences—is problematic (see Chapters 3 & 4). For example, the provision of predictable scheduled adventures (tourism) and assessment against predetermined learning outcomes (education) together illustrate the inseparability of capitalist ideology and the push for economizing effort and resources across all spheres of human endeavour. It is through exposure to adventure activities that individuals, both young and old, have opportunities to construct their identities. It is the 'nature' of these adventures, that school-aged young people are exposed to, that we will discuss in later chapters.

Lynch and Moore's (2004) treatment shows that within adventure's roots in capitalist enterprise, there is scope for reinterpretation and subversion of its existing meanings. As they suggest, "notions of adventure can simultaneously function as both the current manifestation, and entrenchment, of an existing social and economic order and as a means or providing opportunities for new interpretations of personal and social reality" (p. 10). We contend that new interpretations of personal and social reality require a new interpretation of adventure—one that breaks free of existing narrow conceptions and gives students room to explore ideas, movement and emotions in meaningful ways.

'TRUE' ADVENTURE?

Varley (2006) has also drawn attention to the paradoxical aspects of adventure when it is used to refer to predictable or packaged experiences. In an effort to distinguish between adventure as a commodified, predictable product, Varley refers to 'true' or 'original' adventure that he considers to have clear characteristics. Rather than developing an either/or position, he suggests that adventure experiences can be viewed on a continuum: at one end he places commodified products that are sold to consumers who may have few skills and little knowledge of the activity, and at the other end are the participants who are required to use skills developed over time, make decisions relating to risk management and take responsibility for their actions.

As we alluded to earlier, adventures can mean different things to different people, and definitions largely reliant on uncertainty can lead to confusion. Varley's (2006) article attempts to establish some "conceptual anchors for the term 'adventure' that would help to avoid the linguistic relativism that allows everything to mean anything . . . or nothing" (p. 174). As such, his continuum serves as a "contrast-device" (p. 174) against which other ways of thinking about adventure can be considered. He draws on a range of literature from leisure studies, outdoor education, sociology and consumer behaviour to develop an "'ideal' concept of the character of adventure" (p. 175). Varley admits that his ideas are open to challenge and modification and we readily acknowledge that no definition will ever be perfect—not even ours! Yet we also believe that putting a conceptual 'stake in the ground' provides a crucial platform for our discussion.

Drawing on Mortlock's (1984) *The Adventure Alternative*, which was an early attempt to systematically describe a model of adventure experiences, Varley (2006) identified the following four key elements: risk, responsibility, uncertainty and commitment. Following an extensive review of a wide range of material, such as flow (Csikszentmihalyi, 2000); 'edgework' and the desire to glimpse at our own mortality (Lyng, 1990); the quest for existential authenticity (Wang, 1999); and transcendence of the mundane (Macbeth, 2000), Varley identified two different philosophical and ideological traditions concerning the human/nature relationship. The first he referred to as the 'being in and with nature' position, where there was the belief that nature provides an escape from the ills of modern society and a way to return to humankind's true unpolluted condition. The second tradition reflected a view that being in nature was a way to face one's fears, overcome obstacles, develop character and search for authenticity and meaning in one's life. He contends that both of these traditions are evident in contemporary definitions of adventure.

Varley (2006) goes on to suggest that a "definitive, idealised *original* adventure-form emerges only through *commitment* in the face of *uncertainty*, and may be experienced through marginal situations where *risks* may be confronted and overcome by taking *responsibility* for one's actions with minimal recourse to external support systems" (p. 185, original emphasis). In addition, a participant may experience strong emotional responses and may have had a 'flow experience', where one loses oneself in the moment (see Chapter 8). As with the earlier example, in which we cited shopping as a potential adventure activity, it is possible to think of activities that meet these criteria which might not be considered socially desirable, such as theft or illegal use of drugs. Hence any attempt to rigidly define a concept is open to critique and reinterpretation.

Varley's (2006) definition of 'ideal' adventure is precisely that: an idealized version of what he terms "original adventure" (p. 188). He uses this by way of contrast to commodified forms of adventure that are evident in adventure tourism contexts. As we will detail in Chapter 4, we have similar concerns about the commodification of adventure in educational settings. To his credit, Varley recognizes the flaws in such a construct, but the continuum has value in that it helps educators see that labelling an activity as 'adventure education' or 'adventure programming' requires careful scrutiny, rather than the uncontested acceptance of a term that has multiple meanings and which has been applied to heavily commodified, slickly marketed products.

RE-THINKING THE MEANING OF ADVENTURE IN ADVENTUROUS LEARNING

In this chapter we have seen how the word 'adventure' has different meanings for different people. Adventures can be both individually and culturally relative. For example, on an individual level, presenting at an academic conference might be quite daunting for a third year undergraduate student, but it wouldn't be for either of us. The practice of adventuring has been used to build nations (take Norway's quest for the South Pole with Amundsen), cement people's identities as counter-culture risk-takers, 'fix' young people's anti-social behaviour through boot camps and earn huge profits for corporations like The North Face.

Since the word 'adventure' has so many meanings and has been appropriated by so many people, institutions and businesses, it is now too vague for us to use in our discussions—unless, that is, we break it down into four key elements:

- Authenticity (keeping the activities real)
- Agency (ensuring that learners have the power to shape what is learned and how it is learned)
- Uncertainty (being willing to move away from rigid and prescribed processes and allow creativity in finding solutions)

- Mastery (helping learners develop applicable knowledge and skills)

We are mindful of not being overly prescriptive; however, we do not want to leave you trying to read our minds. As individuals who enjoy our own adventures, and who have also participated in commodified adventure tourism experiences, we believe it is important to clearly state that we are concerned with the qualities of adventure in contexts with an overt educational agenda. We are passionate adventurers and equally passionate educators who aim to help you to engage your students more deeply in adventurous experiences which will enable them to benefit more from the learning environments that you are facilitating for them.

In the following chapter, we'll 'zoom out' and examine some of the features of contemporary society that influence both the world of adventure and the world of education—and the fascinating space where they intersect.

Chapter 3

Socio-cultural Backdrop

As intimated in the introductory chapter, curriculum and pedagogy can only be considered, critiqued and designed in relation to the global era and societal norms in which they occur. This is not a new idea, but one that is necessary to state, in terms of establishing the wider context in which this book's themes are located.

For many of us, the world has changed in unrecognizable ways since the time we were children. Consider such diverse topics as the evolution of mobile phones; the myriad ways we can communicate with friends and family; the migration to urban centres (which are increasingly multi-cultural); the contrasting places in which we will work and live during our lifetimes; and the decreasing power that national governments have in relation to multi-national corporations. The rapidity at which these kinds of global changes are taking place is not the only unsettling feature of the times in which we live, as we are also burdened by not knowing the direction in which these changes are travelling. Many of the issues that occupy our time—from trying to update the operating system on our laptop, to attempting to conceive of ways that we might be able to address global climate change—are incredibly complex and changing at a rapid pace.

Central to this chapter is the notion that the speed at which the world is changing is rapidly increasing to a point where the "complexities of the future" are "unknowable" (Robinson, 2011, p. 1). Many of these changes have to do with technology, climate change and shifting demographic patterns. Devising educational programmes for today's young learners that will equip them to flourish in a world undergoing rapid change is clearly a daunting challenge. In order to more effectively teach for a complex and uncertain future, we need to understand more deeply a few basic ideas that characterize the world in which, and for which, we seek to educate.

In this chapter we will:

- Provide an overview of the principal features of late modernity.
- Outline key elements of neo-liberal policies.
- Explain basic aspects of complexity theory.
- Discuss educational discourses in relation to these social phenomena.

LATE MODERNITY, RISK SOCIETIES AND LIQUID TIMES

The period towards the end of the 20th century has been described by some sociologists as *late modernity* (Giddens, 1991). If modernity began with the advent of the industrial age in the mid-1800s, late modernity (for those of us lucky to live in a 'developed' country) is characterized by fast-paced lifestyles, cosmopolitanism, high-tech communications, global mobility, constantly evolving technology and the diminishing 'grand narrative' (Elliot & Urry, 2010; Young, DaRosa & Lapointe, 2011). The grand narrative refers to elements of society that many people used to take for granted as 'right' or desirable. For example, no longer are most of us convinced that a secondary school education will lead to a secure job, with the same company, for one's working life. In times past this was the accepted view of 'how things should be'. These days, of course, jobs come in many forms, people have multiple careers, move across the planet for work, and few of us know what we might be doing in twenty years.

Late modernity is also hallmarked by another big factor, and that is *risk*. During the early 1990s, two prominent sociologists published influential textbooks: The *Consequences of Modernity* (1990) and *Modernity and Self-Identity: Self and Society in the Late Modern Age* (1991) by Anthony Giddens, and *Risk Society* (1992) by Ulrich Beck. Both thinkers contended that people in contemporary western, developed societies were highly focused on insulating themselves from harm. Beck argued that people obsessed about 'minimizing bads' and Giddens explained that we are all preoccupied with the future and with safety. More recently, Bauman (2007) has described contemporary life as 'liquid times' (also the title of the book), where nothing is fixed and humans are dealing with constant insecurity and uncertainty. When compared to people who lived in earlier times, these authors argued that individuals were much less willing to take chances in order to gain something desirable, if this involved the possibility of losing something of value. An important point to keep in mind during our discussion of what Giddens (1991) refers to as the 'risk culture', is that people today are generally healthier, subject to less crime and live longer than at any point in history. What is distinctive about 'our time' is that social life "has become more and more about carving out ways of coping with and managing risk" (Elliot, 2014, p. 305), on both a personal and public level.

Lupton (2013) explains that in medieval times and earlier, life was characterized by insecurity, disease, fear of the night and by natural events that 'disturbed order'. If a member of the family died or one's house was destroyed by fire, there was no recourse to governments or insurance companies or other citizens, as there is today. Long ago, it was customs, beliefs and rituals that were used to mitigate against devastating, unwanted occurrences; there was no talk about risk assessment and risk management.

RISK IN UNCERTAIN TIMES

The term 'risk' was first used in the 1600s in the context of maritime insurance (Lupton, 2013). For example, if sugar or gold was being shipped across an ocean, there were companies that would insure against the risk of losing these goods in a storm. In these early days, the emerging concept of risk excluded human fault and responsibility. Until the industrial age (aka modernity) came along, the 'bads' that needed insuring against were all objective—'acts of God', like a hurricane or a blizzard.

Modernity, with its factories and mills, became synonymous with calculability and control—what Max Weber (1922/1968) labelled *rationalization*. Although Weber outlined four different types of rationalization, the key one was *formal rationality*, which features the means/ends calculations that are such an integral part of capitalism. Because it is objective and focuses on profits, formal rationality often ignores people's needs and wants. And so it was that these newer, more 'modern' ways of thinking assumed that social and natural worlds could be measured, calculated and predicted (Lupton, 2013). All of this measuring, calculating and predicting was done by humans, and, seen in this light, systems working more efficiently (or not working efficiently) was largely a result of human intervention.

The 20th century saw an increase in notions of accountability and, with it, the growing belief that if something bad happened, then it must be somebody's fault. Risk was no longer only concerned with natural events, but with the actions of human beings as well. Fate was no longer an acceptable concept, as "the moderns" had learned to "transform a radically indeterminate cosmos into a manageable one, through the myth of calculability" (Reddy, 1996, p. 237). This notion is problematic, to say the least, as increasingly risks are global, long-term and so complex that they cannot possibly be entirely calculated by science. Take, for example, how the effects of the 2011 tsunami in Japan had consequences far beyond the area that was devastated: the potential for widespread, long-term radio-active contamination had global implications.

Just as we saw with the concept of adventure in Chapter 2, risk is viewed differently by different people. Everyone, from investment bankers to teenaged gang members to backcountry skiers, has a different tolerance of risk. This tolerance, of course, is usually directly proportional to what might be gained by choosing a particular course of action, such as money, social status and psychological thrill.

One final word on risk that needs to be mentioned, is that if you are rich (which, relative to the average inhabitant on planet earth, most readers of this book will be) then you are in luck, as risk is more often a problem for the poor, who cannot afford to insulate themselves against the possibility of being harmed or of losing something of value (Beck, 1992; Lupton, 2013). Even so, risk occupies such a dominant space within social life because not even the wealthiest people "can truly control the cluster of risks which arises today in a world of advanced technology, science and multinational organizations" (Elliot, 2014, p. 304).

Armed with a basic understanding of economic rationalization and some discourses around risk, both features of late modernity, we can now move to the next part of this chapter, which explains the stage upon which our educational practices are set. This section examines the ideas contained within the term neo-liberalism.

NEO-LIBERALISM AND EDUCATION

The term 'neo-liberalism' has found more traction in the United Kingdom (UK) and in Australasia, than it has in North America. It refers to a broad set of ideas that espouse de-regulation in economics, politics, law, religion and many other sectors—the most important of these to us is education. Neo-liberalism came to the fore in the late 1970s and early 1980s, chiefly through the policies of UK prime minister Margaret Thatcher and US president Ronald Reagan. This ideology is hallmarked by the rule of the market and free trade, cutting public expenditure for social services, reducing government regulation, privatization (selling and out-sourcing state businesses and services), and pressuring people to arrange their own health care and education (Martinez & Garcia, 2000). While powerful private-sector influences and leaders on both sides of the political spectrum might argue that neo-liberalism is positive for all, the evidence suggests that this economic liberalism has created "massive economic inequalities among individuals and nations" (Ross & Gibson, 2006, p. 2) and increasing educational inequality (Hursh, 2006).

Less government regulation of major sectors and organizations has several knock-on consequences. First, the government should save money, as it has less to do, in terms of monitoring and accounting for the actions of organizations and businesses that provide services for its people. The second consequence is that the private sector (i.e. for profit companies) has increasing influence and power over citizens' lives. Since these companies operate within a capitalist system, they are justifiably driven by profit-making motives. Charles Taylor (1991) describes this instrumental reasoning as "the kind of rationality we draw on when we calculate the most economical application of means to a given end. Maximum efficiency, the best cost–output ratio, is its measure of success" (p. 5).

While maximizing profit, as a return on investment, might be highly desirable in the world of soap manufacturing, it is less than ideal in the world of education. For us, the principal consequence of neo-liberalism is that market forces have a disproportionately large influence on educational decisions. Too often now, in pre-schools, universities, youth programmes and field study centres, decisions about what is taught, how it is taught, and how it is assessed, are based on economic imperatives, rather than educational ones. In these circumstances, society's aim is to produce "competitive, instrumentally-rational" young people who can compete in the marketplace and be "more productive workers" (Hursh, 2006, pp. 17–18).

Ross and Gibson (2006) explain how neo-liberal legislation has "commodified public education by reducing learning to bits of information and skill to be taught and tested" (p. 4). By relying on economies of scale, class sizes increase, the number of specialists decrease, the curriculum becomes more fixed, testing becomes more standardized and teachers' professional judgments are undermined or restricted (Hursh, 2006). Perhaps the greatest consequence of neo-liberal policies on education has been the advent of standardized testing (Hursh, 2006), which arguably undermines teachers' autonomy and creative capacities, as they are forced to teach students to succeed on universal exams, rather than respond to students' specific learning needs. Using "superficial and decontextualized instruments" to measure ability limits teachers' capacities to see and respond to students' educational needs (Garrison, 1997, p. 186).

Interestingly, there is very limited robust empirical evidence indicating that neo-liberal reforms have improved learning (Ward, 2012). The evidence that does exist suggests that improved test scores have come from schools 'teaching to the test' (see Whitty, 2002). What kind of human beings does this kind of schooling yield? Is the value of what is learned and how it is learned now being driven by market forces? We argue that a broader, more holistic and interdisciplinary education is what today's children need—not one that is narrower.

A Narrowing of Curriculum?

Since the 1970s, an understanding that assessment is what drives student learning has become accepted as conventional wisdom in education circles (Joughin, 2010). Further, high stakes testing has been a major factor in "pushing out non-tested subjects, knowledge, and skills" (Mathis, 2012, p. 3). The argument goes that after a disproportionately large amount of time has been spent on acquiring the skills to succeed on math and language arts tests, there is precious little time to cover vast areas of social studies, for example. This 'narrowing of curriculum' (see Hess & Brigham, 2000; Mathis, 2003) is problematic for four principal reasons.

The first problem is that teachers are left with too many 'less important' aspects of the curriculum to cover in a much shorter period of time (Crocco & Costigan, 2007). One consequence of this "shrinking space" is that it "limits pedagogical options" (p. 513). For many high school teachers, the only feasible way to cover the prescribed curricular ground is by delivering lectures (Crocco & Costigan, 2007). Milner (2014) refers to this as the "scripted curriculum", which makes it difficult for teachers to relate what is being 'taught' to the socio-political realities of human existence. This second problem, of the need for teachers to adopt a lecture style, leads to a third problem: it assumes that this one curriculum will "meet the needs and interests of all students" (Ede, 2006, p. 31). Students are disadvantaged by having to consume a market-driven curriculum that is delivered in a 'one size fits all' manner. This leads to the fourth issue, which is that this kind of education does not involve building relationships between teachers and students, or between students and students (Crocco & Costigan, 2007).

All of these problems have arisen from a model of schooling that is plainly artificial and not designed to provide useful, real-world learning experiences. The 'evils' of preparation for high stakes, standardized tests have severely limited teachers' pedagogical freedom to respond to students' individual needs (Crocco & Costigan, 2007). Education, in this light, has become "a series of prescriptive interventions or steps that deskill teachers and rob students of any possible emotional connection to the subject matter being taught or to the world around them" (Shields, 2012, p. 4). There exists an increasing gap between what can be called the 'planned curriculum' and the 'lived curriculum' (Aoki, 1993). The former is an abstract language "written for faceless people" by officials at state and national levels (p. 261) and is not adept at responding to teachers' and students' uniqueness. In contrast, the latter—the lived curriculum— is "embodied in the very stories and languages people speak and live" (p. 261), and lies at odds with 'systems' of education that are designed for mass consumption.

Robinson (2011) explains how this system of education for the masses continues to directly mirror the factory-like approaches to teaching and learning that hallmarked the industrial age, as it emphasizes "linearity, conformity and standardization" (p. 8). He goes on to remind us that students "are taught broadly the same material and they are assessed against common scales of achievement, with relatively few opportunities for choice or deviation (p. 57). What is surprising is this rather archaic system of education is still being employed in many parts of the world, in an era of rapid change and increasing complexity.

COMPLEXITY

Another important characterizing feature of the time in which we live is its *complexity*. This term was first used by Weaver in 1948, as he explained the difference between simple, complicated and complex systems. A simple system is one where "only a few inert objects or variables interact" (Davis & Sumara, 2006, p. 9), and a complicated system has many parts, but, like a motorcycle, can be dismantled and re-assembled, so that it works in "exactly the same, predictable way" (p. 11). A complex system, however, cannot be taken apart, put back together and then function in the same way. This is so because the individual elements are themselves destroyed when the "relationships between them are broken" (p. 11). Each component of a complex system has a function that relies on multiple, intricate inter-relationships with other components; tweaking one component will influence all others in ways that can be very difficult to predict.

Why are we writing about all of this stuff? Well, as stated earlier in different words, before we can determine the best way to educate, we must deeply understand the kind of world in which we need to educate our students to thrive. We have moved on from the moderns, who believed that the universe was "fixed and fully knowable" (Davis & Sumara, 2006, p. 4) and scientifically explainable through probability and statistics, to a realization that our existence is a complex and constantly changing system that defies "simplistic analyses and cause–effect explanations" (p. xi). It was Fritjof Capra (1997) who explained that society's biggest problems cannot be understood in isolation because they are systemic, where multiple phenomena are interdependent.

This is not all doom and gloom, however, as it is argued that the instability, disequilibrium and unpredictability inherent in complex systems are not only desirable, but required for human survival (Morrison, 2008, p. 21). Indeed, curricula, pedagogical approaches and forms of assessment adopted in many educational settings lack flexibility, and are rigid and unresponsive to the changing world. These outmoded ways of operating fail to provide students with the skills and attributes needed to thrive in 21st-century society.

The implication for educational practice from complexity theorists is that we need to move away from the "over-determined, tidy, traditional, externally mandated and regulated prescriptions" to aid learning (Morrison, 2008, p. 24). The teacher's role needs to shift to that of a facilitator who judiciously creates optimal conditions for learners to "exercise autonomy, responsibility, ownership, self-direction and reflection" (p. 25). But sound education is more than a matter of "behaviour modification", as per 20th-century psycho-educational thinking (Davis & Sumara, 2006, p. 12), or learning content through self-direction. It is part of a complex system that involves various groups of children, parents, teachers, principals, education officers and policy makers who interact in ways that are not predictable (Jess, Atencio & Thorburn, 2011).

Teachers need to engage with learners in a way that features connectivity with the various components within the complex system. Part of this involves 'alerting' the learner to the web of complex relations that they inhabit (Brennan, 1994). Further, it might mean embracing a pedagogy that is at the "edge of chaos" (Jess et al., 2011, p. 195), where young

29

people are learning to adapt themselves to the kinds of diverse circumstances that they will "encounter in a dynamic world" (Davis & Sumara, 2006, p. 14).

Related to this discussion of complexity is the term *VUCA*. VUCA is an acronym for Volatile, Uncertain, Complex and Ambiguous, and is used to describe the rapidly changing world in which we all live. Shields (2012) explains how VUCA was originally developed by the military in the late 1990s, and is creeping into other sectors, such as organizational management and educational leadership.

Those of you who find the subject of complexity interesting will be happy to know that there is also *super complexity*. The term has relevance, as it incorporates elements of late modernity and the risk culture, such as uncertainty, predictability, change and turmoil, more obviously than other descriptions of complexity (Barnett, 2000). The super-complex age is one "in which nothing can be taken for granted" and where "all bets are off" (p. 416). In this article, Barnett is highlighting imperatives for university education in the 21st century, but his words are every bit as appropriate for primary school teachers as they are for youth workers. He calls for an "epistemology for uncertainty" that enables people to develop powers of critical action in an uncertain world (p. 420).

With this collective backdrop of uncertainty, risk and complexity established, we now turn our attention to a discussion of risk as it relates to adventure education and mainstream education, since these are both directly influenced by the socio-cultural themes that we have been exploring.

RISK, ADVENTURE AND EDUCATION

In the earlier section on risk, we noted that the moderns were the first to refute the centuries-old assumption that fate was to blame for anything bad happening. Unsurprisingly, the same appears to be true today, only these cultural attitudes about needing to blame humans for unwanted occurrences have arguably become increasingly engrained, and accepted as normal, over time.

This is particularly apparent in adventure activity programmes with young people, where there seems to be less and less public tolerance of accidents. In the 1970s, for example, there were multiple fatality accidents in the UK and in Canada that did not result in any criminal charges. This changed in 1993, with the Lyme Bay accident in England, which resulted in the first criminal prosecution of an outdoor centre manager.

It also yielded the *Activity Centre (Young Persons' Safety) Act 1995* (http://www.legislation.gov.uk/ukpga/1995/15/contents) and the creation of an inspectorate, which is now called the Adventurous Activities Licensing Service.

Even for those of you who are not adventure-based educators or live in other countries, this bit of history is worth explaining for two reasons. First, it is an example of shifting cultural attitudes towards adventurous activities, in that it was becoming less and less acceptable for young people to die or become seriously injured while outside the classroom on some kind of educational or developmental excursion. And second, it heralded the start of regulated adventurous activities. Regulated adventure is, arguably, an oxymoron.

In the UK, the 1990s and early 2000s marked a time when teachers seemed unwilling to take their students outside the classroom at all, for fear that they might be held accountable for children hurting themselves (Allison & Telford, 2005; Ross, Higgins & Nicol, 2007). School boards with sufficient budgets and an appetite for providing opportunities for adventurous activities did so by having their teachers accompany their students to a licensed residential outdoor centre. Once there, qualified instructors would take over and guide the children through a series of highly prescriptive adventure activities, such as abseiling, canoeing, rope course and orienteering. With the exception of some enlightened centres, there was little focus on curricular learning (e.g., math, geography, history, science), as the emphasis was on building some kind of amorphous personal growth, that was (and still is) virtually impossible to measure— even if it does happen.

This kind of fixed, replicable, predictable view of outdoor education became denuded of adventure; it was no longer an antidote to the pre-scribed world of classroom learning. Indeed, outdoor adventure education was now afflicted with the modern malaise of rationalization that was discussed earlier in the chapter.

However, it is arguable that the tide has turned somewhat and in 2015 (in Scotland in particular) there is a shift back towards supporting what a reasonable and prudent teacher might do with their class. More crucially, there is a growing concern that children who are denied education outside of the classroom experiences, are effectively being robbed of the rich array of real-world learning experiences to which they are entitled (see Beames, Atencio & Ross, 2009).

In terms of physical sites for a child's learning and development, the safest environment might arguably be in a classroom with no chairs and tables, and padded walls and floors. Such an arrangement might minimize some 'bads', but at the same time it would probably severely limit the acquisition of any 'goods'. This discussion becomes more interesting as we dig deeper into where the crossroad lies between an educational environment that is stimulating, invigorating and full of useful learning, but one that does not put the student at risk of encountering any artificial or unreasonable hazard.

A space for learning that inhabits a world between the padded, furnitureless classroom and the south col of Mount Everest, is what we seek. As we shall see in Chapter 5, the richest sites for contextualized and authentic learning are often 'out there', in the real world. There is certainly no reason why children, as part of our educational programmes, cannot be justifiably exposed to many of the same hazards that they might encounter while on their own, outside of school hours (Gill, 2010). One could argue that teachers have a duty to manage developmentally appropriate encounters with common, everyday hazards, such as crossing roads. Encounters with hazards faced by people in general—and learning to assess the likelihood and severity of being harmed by them—are a part of every life outside of schooling, and should be a natural part of an education that takes place in the real world (Beames, Higgins & Nicol, 2011).

SUMMARY

We know that for many educators, "the world we live in is vastly different from the one in which many of us developed" (Irwin, Straker & Hill, 2012, p. 12). More importantly, for both us and our students, the world of the future will be vastly different than today's, and different in some ways that we cannot even imagine, let alone predict.

We find it somewhat amusing that here we are, writing about educational reform in 2015, when so many have expounded on this before. Since the 1930s, Kurt Hahn, Paulo Freire and Maria Montessori—to name three quite contrasting educational visionaries—have rooted their work in the geo-political and socio-cultural challenges of their times. Dewey was no different, in that he saw the progressive education movement as part of a wider response to the "increasingly corrosive social, economic, and psychological order brought about by industrial capitalism" (Seaman & Nelsen, 2011, p. 6). Certainly, there is a growing number of educational critics (e.g., Ross & Gibson, 2006; Robinson, 2011) who fear that political agendas and consumer society together drive educational policy towards outcomes that are clearly measurable, but which in turn limit schools' capacities to help their students develop into 'full' human beings (Bonnett & Cuypers, 2002).

This chapter has provided an overview of the key features of late modernity, the 'risk culture', neo-liberalism and complexity. The ideas contained within these features together provide a backdrop upon which our educational practices take place. Whatever we do as part of our teaching provision does not happen in an isolated vacuum; on the contrary, our educational practices are highly influenced by the various social, cultural, economic and political contexts that we've outlined. As educators who aim to improve student learning, we need to understand these contexts in order to more effectively design and deliver classes that are conducted within them.

Uncertain times and neo-liberal, market-driven forces have conspired to leave educational practice predictable, uninspiring, made for the masses. This paradox is shameful, as the ever-changing times in which we live demand young people who can develop capacities and find effective solutions to complex, fluid, problems that may not even currently exist. Yet, the dominant educational paradigm teaches in a way that lies in ideological opposition to the way the world works. Today's education needs to respond to students' individual needs, as they, through their education, respond to the problems that they encounter through their own journey.

This overview of the social backdrop that shapes how humans feel, think and act in the late modern age provides the platform from which we can examine current adventure education practice, which is the focus of the next chapter.

Chapter 4

Adventure Education, Rationalization and Commodification

Adventure education, featuring challenging outdoor activities with an accompanying rhetoric based in discourses of inclusion, student-centred learning, problem-based learning and experiential education, has much to offer students and teachers alike. It is clear that a carefully structured and well-thought-out programme with a sound educational rationale can support student engagement and learning. *Carefully structured, well-thought-out, with a sound educational rationale.* These are three key phrases that should underpin the provision of all adventure education experiences. Based on our observations, however, we fear that the allure of fun activities that keep students 'busy and happy' may actually undermine both the stated goals of adventure education (improvement in personal and social spheres) and practitioners' good intentions about it being an alternative to mainstream schooling. We would go further and suggest that some adventure programmes actually reinforce the neo-liberal and consumerist discourses they claim to be opposing.

If you're not particularly interested in adventure education, this chapter may have less relevance to your practice. Therefore, please feel free to skip ahead to Chapter 5. In the sections that follow we will pick up on some of the issues that have been raised in Chapters 2 and 3 (the meanings of adventure and the social backdrop) and discuss them in relation to learning through adventure. The three inter-related areas of concern that we will examine are:

- The increasing commodification of adventure education and the implications of this for participant learning.

- The misplaced popularity of thrilling/novel activities containing an element of risk, which encourages passivity in students and marginalizes the role of educators.
- The increasingly contested assumption that what is learned in novel settings is readily transferable to students' everyday lives.

COMMODIFICATION

As detailed in Chapter 3, rationalization has seen the "systematic, measured application of science to work and everyday life" (Varley, 2013, p. 35). Evidence of the encroachment of rationalizing processes into adventure education has been documented by a number of writers (Loynes, 2013; Roberts, 2012; Varley, 2013). They give examples such as the advent of national governing bodies and instructor qualifications. Associated with rationalizing processes, which have been central to the efficient production of goods and the supply of services, is the notion of commodification. Commodification refers to the process "by which the value of goods or services is not only understood in terms of the intrinsic benefits they provide, but also, or often exclusively, for the extrinsic value (such as money) that can be made for the provision" (Loynes, 2013, p. 138). As discussed briefly in Chapter 2, white-water rafting and sky-diving are examples of commodified adventure experiences in the tourism sector. As commercial activities, it is hardly surprising that these experiences are packaged and sold to consumers as a commodity. We maintain that many of the same principles apply when it comes to the provision of adventure education experiences for school-age children. Seen this way, students are increasingly being positioned as consumers rather than learners.

Several authors (Beames & Brown, 2014; Loynes, 1998, 2013; Roberts, 2012) have drawn attention to the commodification of adventure experiences in education. In the sections that follow we draw attention to some of the processes that have been identified to help explain how commodification is evidenced in practice.

MCDONALDIZATION

Loynes (1998) drew on Ritzer's (1993) concept of McDonaldization to examine how outdoor education experiences were becoming market driven, highly commodified, and were in "danger of allowing the market to do to outdoor adventure what it has done elsewhere, that is to disassociate people from their experience of community and place" (p. 35).

Loynes' influential paper entitled *Adventure in a Bun* was inspired by Ritzer's thesis on the McDonaldization of society, whereby "much of life's experiences are increasingly provided as standard, dependable, and safe products just like the McDonald's hamburger" (1998, p. 35). Ritzer argued that the McDonald's fast-food franchise provided an exemplary model of the rationalization of goods and services. His framework sought to explain the broader economic circumstances that were compelling businesses to rationalize their products in order to decrease costs and increase profits. The McDonaldization framework explains how more and more companies are focusing on increasing the efficiency, calculability, predictability and control of the products they are selling, while replacing human labour with technology wherever possible.

The drive for *efficiency* puts a focus on achieving intended outcomes with less cost and energy. The second feature is *calculability*, or the increasing emphasis that is placed on quantifying operations. The principle of calculability ensures that decisions on how goods or services will be provided will be based on cost–benefit calculations. The third feature of Ritzer's framework is *predictability*. As Beames and Brown (2014) explain, a company can lose income through unexpected events, therefore it will try and control as many factors as possible in order to minimize disruption to production and sales. For some providers, keeping events as predictable as possible means moving outdoor activities, such as skiing and climbing, indoors (Bottenburg & Salome, 2010).

Ritzer's (1993) fourth feature, *control*, refers to the power an organization exercises over its employees and customers. This may be in the form of a dress code, points of entry and exit from facilities or the nature of the interaction between staff and customers. The final feature of McDonaldization is the replacement of human labour with technology. Modern organizations increasingly use automation in place of people (e.g., ATM machines replace bank tellers).

A good example of McDonaldization in adventure education is the challenge course (also known as the high ropes course). These courses are intended to provide exciting experiences for participants in a tightly controlled environment. The courses are designed and constructed so that staff can survey participants from strategic vantage points, and the elements flow so that participants can be moved efficiently through the course. The design of the course allows for specific entry and exit points and participant numbers are controlled so that the amount of time to complete the course can be determined. Equipment is supplied and the clothing that can be worn is regulated (often with recourse to issues of safety). Many challenge ropes courses have also replaced human belayers (people who control the safety rope) with automated or 'closed-loop' systems, which means that the human input into safety has now been automated. Organizational protocols and operating procedures determine staff positions within the courses, provide scripts for safety briefings and extend to how the experiences might be facilitated to maximize learning.

Loynes (1998, 2002) has highlighted how mechanistic/production language has even permeated how learning from these experiences might be facilitated (e.g., the use of the term 'processing'). More recently, Loynes (2013) recalled witnessing the construction of the first ropes course in India, which aimed to replicate the same training methods available in the USA or Europe. A challenge ropes course is an excellent exemplar of efficiency, calculability, predictability, control and increasing automation in action across a range of geographical areas and user groups.

McDonaldization was Ritzer's (1993) attempt to explain a process of commodification in an increasingly globalized economy. A subsequent, and complementary process, was proffered by Bryman (1999), who coined the phrase Disneyization to explain trends in how goods and services are supplied.

DISNEYIZATION

Disneyization refers to application of the principles of Disney theme parks to other enterprises. Bryman (2004) identified four principles: theming, hybrid consumption, merchandising and performative labour. *Theming* refers to the way in which a service is provided so that it becomes an 'immersive experience' with a high degree of coherence. For example, a restaurant's name hints at the style of food, the décor and the music that might be played (e.g., The Hard Rock Café). Irish pubs are an excellent example of this phenomenon; whether in Canada or New Zealand, all customers are 'transported' to an idealized slice of Ireland.

The second principle of Disneyization is *hybrid consumption*. This can be understood as the blurring of lines between 'playing' and 'purchasing'. For example, at Legoland you can buy Lego products in between rides and then return to the Legoland hotel. Hybrid consumption describes how seemingly unrelated activities (e.g., playing, eating, sleeping and buying souvenirs) are "inextricably interwoven" (Bryman, 1999, p. 34).

The third principle is *merchandising*. Starbucks Coffee provides a good example. In addition to buying a cup of coffee, customers are enticed with French presses, CDs, mugs, cups, flasks and bags of coffee, that are all available for purchase. Quite often these are marketed adjacent to where you wait for your coffee. In some businesses it is the themed merchandise that provides a stream of income which is equal to or exceeds that from the primary business activity (Bryman, 1999). The final principle is *performative labour*.[1] Performative labour requires employees to exhibit "cheerfulness and friendliness towards customers as part of the service encounter" (Bryman, 1999, p. 39). While it is reasonable to expect people to behave in a polite manner, performative behaviour takes this a step further with the advent of 'greeters' and assistants who follow prescribed scripts (e.g., the 'have a nice day' is issued to all customers).

COMMODIFICATION IN THE PROVISION OF ADVENTURE EDUCATION EXPERIENCES

In an earlier paper (Beames & Brown, 2014), we examined the provision of 'outdoor' experiences in Scotland and New Zealand by using the principles briefly outlined above. While the McDonaldization of adventure education has been highlighted (Loynes, 1998, 2013; Roberts, 2012), there was little evidence of the principles of Disneyization being examined. In our study we visited two indoor climbing centres and two indoor ski slopes located in Scotland and New Zealand. Employing the lens of Disneyization we found evidence of the principles discussed above. Without being unnecessarily repetitive we will briefly illustrate how these were evidenced.[2]

Theming was evidenced in multiple ways, from the naming of the cafes/restaurants (e.g., Belay Café, 7 Summits Bar), to the décor (faux fireplace and skis mounted on the wall), to the children's climbing area that featured characters from theme-related storybooks and movies. These examples reinforce Bryman's (2004) point that, by "infusing objects with meaning through theming, they are deemed to be more attractive and interesting than they would otherwise be" (p. 15).

Hybrid consumption was also evident, but less so than one might find in more developed destination-style theme parks. All sites offered food and the opportunity to purchase related items of equipment. The two snow slopes had the most extensive offerings, including conference facilities, bars, restaurants and retail outlets. Both also offered visits to see and be photographed with Santa in the snow during December (a bizarre concept, given it was summer time in New Zealand). The ski centre in Scotland provided the best example of hybrid consumption, as it is located within a larger leisure complex where there were at least 10 retail stores, 15 food outlets, mini-golf and cinemas.

Merchandising was evident at some sites, with branded mugs, water bottles and t-shirts. Some providers did not supply 'self-branded' products, but instead sold established brands associated with the lifestyle image they wished to portray (e.g., Burton t-shirts). One more recent development that we noted was the extensive use of social media to connect with customers and to inform them of special deals or upcoming events—all of which would give past customers more reasons to return and spend.

The final principle, performative labour, was the least evident aspect of Bryman's thesis. We did not receive a formulaic equivalent of "would you like fries with that?" we did, however, observe staff embodying some of the attributes of their outdoor counterparts: the easygoing demeanour and mannerisms of the rope tow operators was similar to that displayed by 'lifties' in Australasia or North America, and staff in the rock climbing centres dressed in a way that stated, "I'm a climber" rather than, "I'm a service worker in a largely repetitive job". We noted that,

> The instructors at Extreme Edge projected the demeanour of the 'expert', as they sauntered around wearing a climbing harness and, despite asking if you had any climbing experience and hearing the answer 'yes', launched into a demonstration of how to use the belay device. There was no sign of any specific, personal deference, as all customers are treated equally; no one's competence is assessed. Clearly, they were following one 'blanket' script to ensure that customers had received instruction.
>
> (Beames & Brown, 2014, p. 124)

Adventure education appears to be sliding down the same slippery slope of so many other aspects of consumer society. There appears to be a trend towards adventure recreation/education activities being offered in increasingly Disneyized settings, where visitors can eat, play and shop under one roof.

IMPLICATIONS OF COMMODIFIED ADVENTURE EDUCATION EXPERIENCES

Granted, the four sites that we examined in our study were not created for the prime purpose of education. As business enterprises they would have been established to cater for a range of clients and interests (e.g., recreation, fitness, skill acquisition, corporate training). The diversification of offerings, with the cafés, merchandising and conference facilities alongside the activities themselves, provide alternative income streams that

39

make 'business sense'. However, during our visits we observed groups of school children using the facilities as part of the extended school curriculum. As commercial enterprises, investors would be looking to maximize their return on investment and, understandably, the rationalizing processes that pervade western modes of operating would underpin how these businesses operate.

These four facilities provide adventure experiences that feature many of the hallmarks of commodification that have been highlighted by Ritzer (1993) and Bryman (1999, 2004). They are all located in an enclosed environment, thus eliminating variables in the weather, while constraining the physical space in which participants can engage with each other and members of staff. These enclosed spaces, with a range of ways to spend money, enable businesses to "create predictable and efficient environments for the consumption of experiences and goods" (Beames & Brown, 2014, p. 124). In our earlier paper we asked, *What might be the implications for learners when adventure experiences are conducted in settings that show the hallmarks of McDonaldization and Disneyization?* We responded thus:

> These types of outdoor recreation/education provision situate educators and learners within a model that Edwards and Corte (2010, p. 1135) have labelled 'mass market commercialization', where the producers (the adventure centre and its staff) and the primary consumers (the school children) are physically distanced from outdoor climbing and skiing/snowboarding sites. Experiences are delivered in a predictable and calculable manner with the intent to maximize efficiency. This ensures the minimization of risk (financial and physical) and the maximization of customer satisfaction and return on investment (both time and monetary). For teachers with busy workloads and an increasingly crowded curriculum, the use of such providers appears sensible. However, returning to Loynes' original critique, we ask: what messages are conveyed in the decision to opt for provision of this nature? How does this impact on student learning?
>
> (Beames & Brown, 2014, p. 124)

We think it is important to highlight several potential ways that student learning is influenced. First, it would appear that programmes in environments where students are positioned as consumers of a product offer limited opportunities for students to take responsibility for their actions, and thus have more in common with an amusement park than with an educational endeavour (Hunt, 1990a). These highly contrived settings, with fancy lighting, music and appealing imagery might provide students with a fun and enjoyable consumer experience, but "Little in the way of growth and learning opportunities are afforded in such artificial situations that in effect, do not require significant decision-making by the learner, and thus no ownership of consequences" (Brown & Fraser, 2009, p. 70).

This discussion of adventures with no significant decision-making is of particular interest to us. Rubens (1999) distinguished between two kinds of adventure: narrow and broad. Narrow adventures feature short timescales, high thrills, minimal participant effort, with few responsibilities devolved to students (e.g., the zip wire). Broad adventures, unsurprisingly, are characterized by long timescales, varied challenges, sustained effort demanded of the participant and increased responsibilities for decision-making given to students. Rubens also discussed the idea of mastery, which we will address in Chapter 8.

Brown and Fraser (2009) also suggest that activities conducted in highly controlled environments may prevent participants from developing autonomy because learners are enveloped in a "network of technologies" comprising safety equipment, fixed procedures and a mechanistic sequencing of activities (p. 71). Becker (2008) echoes this point and argues that the commodification of adventure activities results in the removal of authentic decision-making that restricts learning.

> What remains . . . are some tickling and thrilling feelings. This sort of standardization insinuates that an adventure always functions the same way, as routines do. Those who are dragged through these programmes have to give up their autonomy. They are transformed into a part of the technocratically organized and reproducible process.
>
> (Becker, 2008, p. 208)

We believe that learning is a more complex and 'messy' undertaking than simply doing a series of activities and expecting all students to have learned the intended lessons. The highly commodified provision of activities, such as a rock-climbing session or ski lesson in an indoor setting, conveys a set of messages that experiences are to be consumed, connections to the natural environment are irrelevant, and the histories of particular recreational pastimes can be ignored; furthermore, the vagaries of the weather are eliminated and the original purpose of an activity is largely lost. Roberts (2012) argues that experiences themselves become consumable products, whereby pleasure is available through any one of a number of activities. He suggests that behind the appealing rhetoric of choice, autonomy and responsibility lies the insidious influence of rationalization and commodification:

> Presented with 'experiences' and 'choices' and 'autonomy', they will happily comply, all the while never realizing that such experiences have been carefully planned and selected *for them*. Yes, you can have it 'your way', it's just that 'your way' and 'our way' turn out to be the same thing.
>
> (p. 95)

Roberts (2012) goes on to comment that the philosophical roots of experiential education, which underpin adventure education, are lauded as being "subversive to the dominant mode of schooling . . . [yet] in its technical application it becomes quite innocuous and functionalist" (p. 97). Rather than being an alternative to mainstream schooling practices (see Loynes, 1998), adventure education can become part of the problem that it set out to subvert: students are not empowered, they perform skills that are abstracted from the 'real world', and they have little opportunity to display initiative, to experiment and to take responsibility for their actions. The power differentials of the classroom (teacher–student) are perpetuated in these tightly controlled adventures (instructor/expert–student; producer–consumer).

One of the other issues hidden in the provision of commodified adventures, whether they be indoors or at specially constructed outdoor settings (e.g., the rappelling tower, artificial rock wall), is the marginalization of the environment and the lack of opportunities for students to forge connections with the natural world. Louv (2008) has explained how this sustained and normalized disconnection can result in what he termed "nature deficit disorder". While we prefer not to diagnose a disorder, we are very mindful of the value of positive experiences in and with nature for a person's health and well-being (see, for example Roly Russell et al., 2013). Developing relationships with the natural world may encourage an ethic of care for the environment that has been missing in many industrialized nations (Wattchow & Brown, 2011). The provision of activities in highly fabricated environments (e.g., the sites we studied or in purpose-built challenge courses outdoors) relegates the natural world to an incidental or controllable variable. This perpetuates ideas of the natural world as a resource to be modified or consumed, which is counter to the early aims of adventure educators, which were to develop the skills, knowledge and attitudes required to travel through natural environments.

The importance of 'where' learning occurs has been the subject of much discussion (Gruenewald, 2003; Gruenewald & Smith, 2008; Wattchow & Brown, 2011). What is agreed is that the places where we learn, and our relationship with them, play a huge role in enabling and constraining what is learned. Gruenewald (2003) states that, "places teach us about how the world works and how our lives fit into spaces that we occupy. Further, places make us: As occupants of particular places with particular attributes, our identity and our possibilities are shaped" (p. 621).

A bush or coastal walk provides a very different set of experiences to those provided at an indoor rock-climbing centre or ski slope; thus, places of learning are not 'neutral'. There is no such thing as a 'context-free' learning outcome. Personal and social development outcomes, which are often the focus of adventure education, are heavily intertwined with where learning occurs. By 'side-lining' the environment to provide a commodified experience, we do our students a disservice. Where we educate is critically important, as places structure what is experienced and how it is experienced. Places shape what is learned and convey particular messages about what is valued. The processes of commodification shape student learning in powerful and complex ways that are not always immediately apparent.

THE ACTIVITY FOCUS IN ADVENTURE EDUCATION

Standing atop a wobbly pole 10 metres above the ground and being encouraged to jump into space in order to touch a ball suspended just out of reach, is enough to get one's heart racing, have a moment of doubt about the strength of the equipment, and hope like hell the people on the safety line are concentrating. Leaping from the pole into the void provides a thrill, an adrenaline kick, occasional tears (joy and fear) and a sense of satisfaction. It is an example of one of many activities that use technical equipment and artificial settings to take people outside their 'comfort zone' in the name of learning. This element of a ropes course, known variously as the leap of faith or pamper pole, heightens a participant's perception of risk while keeping the real risk at a low level. Participants wear full body harnesses and are connected to two safety lines that are controlled by an instructor or other participants under direct supervision.

These types of activities are common in many countries and have become routine features of adventure education. However, questions remain about why these 'artificial' and highly contrived activities have so thoroughly permeated international adventure education practice. One possible reason is the intersection between discourses of risk and the need to commodify experiences. We have provided an explanation of the commodification of adventure and the implications for student engagement. We also think it is worth briefly discussing some of the less obvious problems that arise when activities involving heightened physical risk are used to push people outside their comfort zones so that they will learn.

The use of risk has been embraced as a central pillar and distinguishing characteristic of adventure education (Miles & Priest, 1990, 1999; Priest & Gass, 1997; Wurdinger, 1997). Indeed, Wurdinger has suggested that risk "is the element that distinguishes adventure education from other educational fields" (p. 43). Risk has been defined as "the potential to lose something of value. The loss may lead to physical (broken bones), mental (psychological fear), social (peer embarrassment) or financial harm (lost or damaged equipment) . . . Risk is created from the presence of dangers" (Priest, 1999, p. 113). The use of risk as a pedagogical tool is premised on the belief that students will learn when placed in a situation that requires them to step outside their comfort zone, overcome a fear, or extend themselves through an undertaking a challenging task. While some students might respond positively to being challenged and being placed in situations outside their comfort zone, this is not always the case (Brown, 2008; Leberman & Martin, 2003; Wolfe & Samdahl, 2005). A strong body of evidence from the field of positive psychology suggests that the greatest amount of change comes when participants feel safe, secure and accepted (Davis-Berman & Berman, 2002). Davis-Berman & Berman have argued that,

> more productive avenues to growth and change exist, based on participants' safety and security. The paradigm shift suggested . . . reflects a movement toward a more intrinsic model of motivation to change. This model is based on emotional safety and stability in programs, rather than an emphasis on increasing risk and moving out of comfort zones.
>
> (p. 310)

Loynes (2002) has commented that the commodification of risk in the provision of adventure experiences and the "dominance of the voice of this paradigm" has popularized the belief that this is the "only one way or, perhaps a right way to do things" (p. 113). In the sections above we have seen how commodification, as part of the rationalizing process, has permeated the provision of adventure activities. One of the advantages to the adventure 'industry' (and we use the term intentionally) of the 'naturalness' of activities involving risks (height, steep ground or moving water) is the requirement for experienced and skilled instructors to manage the risks. If physical risk taking is seen as a natural and integral part of adventure education, then keeping students safe demands that expert technicians are employed to facilitate these activities. This process of rationalization has many winners: national governing bodies, curriculum developers and qualifications auditors, tertiary education providers, specialist outdoor providers, contract instructors and of course young people who might want a career in the outdoors. There are, however, also some who stand to 'lose' from these developments. We would argue that these include teachers who no longer feel equipped to provide safe outdoor learning opportunities (because they are led to believe 'real' outdoor activities involve high ropes, abseiling and kayaking), and students from lower socio-economic backgrounds, who cannot afford the extra costs associated with employing specialist staff, or the transport costs needed to get to 'wilderness' settings. Let us be very clear: we fervently believe that the emphasis on activities involving physical risk has the undesirable effect of constraining learning for all students.

Brown and Fraser (2009) have argued that the emphasis on activities involving risk and the need to actively manage it has resulted in a 'one-way' form of instruction where, due to the risks inherent in the activity, the instructor is required to tell, direct and establish the rules for participation. This aspect of adventure education pedagogy has been observed by Hovelynck (2001), who argued that "adventure education is increasingly adopting the didactic teaching methods that it set out to be an alternative for" (p. 4). In the didactic or 'one-way' transmissive model, the learner's role is to listen, comply and follow instructions, under the assumption that 'risk experts' are able to provide experiences for the learner's growth and development. Such an assumption presumes that learning is a one-way process where what is taught—is what people learn (Brown & Fraser, 2009).

Given the element of risk that is inherent in activities involving height, steep ground or moving water, the expert is required to take a very hands-on and, at times, directive approach. Brown and Fraser (2009) argue that activities requiring active management strategies and expert inter-vention,

can undermine internal decision-making and learners' sense of agency. The contrived nature of many risk-oriented activities that are highly orchestrated provide learners with a 'do' or 'not do' binary. Either they take the risk (and hopefully succeed) or do not (and are found wanting). Little in the way of growth and learning opportunities are afforded in such artificial situations that in effect, do not require significant decision-making by the learner, and thus no ownership of consequences.

(p. 70)

Brown and Fraser (2009) go on to explain that typical adventure-based activities require risk to be managed by experts, which prevents "participants from engaging in, developing and extending complex risk-taking strategies of their own volition, albeit in supported circumstances" (p. 71). This arrangement potentially limits the "development of autonomy or resilience by the removal of natural consequences due to the need to manage risk" (p. 71).

If we are serious about giving students opportunities to develop autonomy, to learn from their mistakes, and to take responsibility for their actions, then we might consider alternative adventure activities to those that readily come to mind. Take, for example, the challenge ropes course: it is not possible to allow students to experiment with different ways of wearing a harness or to see what happens if they let go of a belay rope, as the consequences do not allow for initiative to be exercised in this setting. On the contrary, we tell students how to wear a harness, where they can and cannot stand, what actions are acceptable on certain elements, and how to belay (in which case they are taught to obediently follow instructions like robots).

We agree with Beedie and Bourne (2005), who have argued that the debate around risk needs to be moved from a focus on "risk activities *per se*" (p. 338) to a broader understanding of education that prioritizes holistic and democratic learning. The final point that we will make in this chapter relates to the assumption that what is learnt during adventure education programmes can easily be transferred to other aspects of students' lives.

ADVENTURE EDUCATION AND TRANSFER TO EVERYDAY LIFE

One of the biggest challenges for educators, irrespective of the subject area, is the extent to which what is learnt in one context is applicable in other contexts (Brown, 2010). Many adventure education texts refer to the ability for people to repeat a skill or apply knowledge across a range of contexts as transfer (Priest & Gass, 1997; Priest, Gass & Gillis, 2000;

Sugarman, Doherty, Garvey & Gass, 2000). Transfer has been described as "one of the most critical features of adventure programming" (Priest & Gass, 2005, p. 21). Dickson and Gray (2006) stated that, "Facilitating experiences that are indelible, transferable and meaningful is the cornerstone of experiential and outdoor learning" (p. 51). The desire to ensure that transfer occurs has resulted in the development of multiple generations of facilitation techniques which are aimed at extracting and embedding key learning outcomes.

Adventure educators have used a number of approaches to facilitating learning, from the simple "let the mountains speak for themselves approach" (i.e., the experience is sufficiently powerful that learners will be able to make sense of it on their own), to discussions post-activity where students are encouraged to make connections to their lives beyond the outdoor setting, to advanced techniques with the use of metaphors and 'double-binds'. In their 2007 book, Gass and Stevens identified eight generations of increasingly sophisticated approaches to foster transfer. It is not unreasonable for readers to ask, *Why has there been a need to develop increasingly sophisticated approaches to facilitating transfer?* Well, perhaps transfer of learning is not as straightforward as some advocates of adventure education would have us believe. For example, why is it that even if a student displays teamwork and care for others during a camp experience, they may not necessarily do this back at school?

Clearly, one solution to this problem has been to develop increasingly sophisticated tools to promote learning, while another equally problematic solution has been to 'up the ante' and make the activities more thrilling, higher, faster—in the hope that they will leave a deeper 'imprint' on the individual. We have seen how the latter solution has resulted in the use of technically advanced activities that marginalize the teacher's input, disadvantage students from some socio-economic backgrounds and diminish opportunities for all students to be creative, take responsibility for their actions and develop higher levels of autonomy.

We would suggest that there is a more fundamental issue at play here: the problematic issue of transfer itself. In a paper examining the assumptions underpinning challenge ropes course practices, Wolfe and Samdahl (2005) noted that providers had a strong belief in transfer of learning as an outcome of participation. They explained how practitioners "adamantly cling to their belief that challenge interventions produce long-term change in individuals" (p. 39) despite a lack of supporting evidence. In a 2010 paper, Brown examined the literature on transfer and drew the conclusion that not only is transfer hard to define, but it is also difficult to investigate.

In the words of Packer (2001), transfer is "perplexingly controversial" (p. 493). There is a high degree of ambiguity in the research findings and little empirical evidence to support the notion of transfer (Detterman, 1993).

Brown (2010) concluded that educators' attempts to justify the value of adventure education "through recourse to transfer and the development of increasingly sophisticated facilitation techniques remains problematic and will continue to be so because of some underlying misconceptions about the nature of learning, transfer and behavioural predictability" (p. 20). Seen this way, claims about students learning teamwork or trust from participation in a ropes course session or the solving of an initiative problem should be taken with a 'pinch of salt'.

Fun and enjoyable activities can be memorable and can have an impact on a person's sense of self-worth, but these possible outcomes are highly contingent upon a range of factors, such as individual motivation, opportunities to repeat these behaviours in similar contexts, and peer support. Learning is a 'messy affair' and there is not a linear relationship between what might be experienced, the behaviours that one might display and long-term learning. In fact, lessons learned in adventure activities that contrast too sharply with one's everyday life can be dismissed as being irrelevant in other contexts or as being of entertainment value only (Brown, 2010).

SUMMARY

At this point in the chapter you may be a little perplexed about why we are still advocates of learning through adventure—after all, the last few thousand words have apparently undermined some of the bases of much outdoor adventure education practice. What we have endeavoured to do is to illustrate that what is often called 'adventure education' does not necessarily involve students in meaningful adventurous learning endeavours. Through the processes of rationalization, adventures have been commodified and highly regulated: students may be given a brief adrenaline buzz and have fun, but they are given limited opportunities for experimentation and ownership of learning.

Our aim is to reclaim the term adventure and provide you with different ways to challenge existing practices. What if we were to offer more student-directed activities that involved less physical risk, which in turn enabled more experimentation and student leadership? What if the activities connected to the students 'out of school lives' and they could do these on a regular basis with friends and family, rather than needing an expert instructor and technical equipment? What if students didn't have to travel to an outdoor centre or a wilderness area to have stimulating experiences outdoors? These 'what ifs' situate adventures closer to the everyday lives of students, their teachers and their communities. Thus, the need for transfer of learning to bridge a gap is lessened. One-off experiences could be replaced with on-going involvement and learning-through-doing.

At this stage of the book, we have discussed the multiple meanings of the word 'adventure' and we have provided an overview of social theories that explain how our lives (and forms of education) are influenced by the features of late modernity. We have also highlighted the key criticisms of conventional adventure education practice. Armed with this knowledge, we now turn towards the second section of the book, which outlines the four dimensions of adventurous learning that can be adopted and adapted as you craft ways to facilitate other people's learning. These dimensions are: Authenticity, Agency, Uncertainty and Mastery.

NOTES

1   In his 1999 paper, Bryman used the term "emotional labour".
2   See the original paper for a fuller treatment of these issues.

Chapter 5

Authenticity

Going outside in one's local neighbourhood may not seem as adventurous as taking part in adrenaline-pumping outdoor activities, but there is a growing body of research that shows that localized programmes, that connect with the everyday lives of learners, can provide stimulating and engaging contexts for learning (Beames & Ross, 2010; Brown, 2012a, 2012b; Fägerstam, 2014; Mannion, Fenwick & Lynch, 2013). For a range of learners (primary, secondary and tertiary level) exploring a local neighbourhood can offer a "higher degree of authentic adventure than highly regulated ropes course and rock climbing sessions that are common at traditional residential outdoor centres" (Beames & Ross, 2010, p. 106). One of the key aspects of more localized programmes is that they connect learners to the physical and social worlds that they inhabit. Such programmes have a greater level of authenticity, as they connect learning to the everyday lives of the participants.

In this chapter we will:

- Explain the difference between 'inert' or 'busy work' and meaningful educational endeavours.
- Introduce the fundamental arguments for contextualizing learning experiences.
- Outline the rationale for place- and community-based education.
- Define what we mean by the term authenticity and discuss the importance of continuity, which involves linking students' present learning to their past experiences, in order to prepare them for the future.

When we discuss matters of authenticity, we are generally talking about what feels real to us: who we are, where we are, who we are with, what we are doing and why we are doing it. What is authentic is usually thought to be of the highest standard, and less authentic things are often perceived of as lower quality and less desirable—just compare a genuine Rolex watch with a cheap copy bought from a street vendor. Authentic items often take a long time to make, are constructed with care, patience and expertise, and often cost more than their mass-produced counterparts. Likewise, authentic experiences are those in which we need to make an investment of time and energy, display commitment, and where we have control over the process and outcome, such as a weekend family canoe trip, as opposed to a visit to an amusement park.

Although this chapter's chief concern is authentic learning environments, we would be remiss if we did not also consider the authenticity of the individual learner herself. In Taylor's (1991) words, authenticity is about "following a voice of nature within us" (p. 27). Implicit in Taylor's writing is the idea that people are 'free' when they make decisions about their lives that are not overly shaped by external influences. The links to a person's agency and autonomy (examined in Chapter 6) are quite obvious. Taylor (1991) claims that each of us has a particular "way of being" (p. 28), and that finding this way involves seizing one's potential to discover and define oneself.

If authenticity is about what is 'real', it follows that authenticity in education is concerned with learning that takes place in the real world and which can be usefully applied in everyday life. This applies to the setting, the content, the methods and the learning outcomes. Ultimately, "authentic concerns" are our "bridge to a personally meaningful world" (Bonnett & Cuypers, 2002, p. 331). This meaning is created by individuals expressing themselves and "feeling the world's response" (p. 331) to material they are motivated to learn about, because to them it possesses a certain integrity and relevance.

The teacher's chief focus, then, should be on "the engagement of the learners with whatever seriously occupies them" and not on some "prespecified piece of knowledge" (Bonnett & Cuypers, 2002, p. 339). They suggest that the content should not be organized around externally imposed frameworks nor on someone else's rationality. This seems like rather radical thinking to us, as it questions the role of the teacher. Still, this sentiment strongly resonates with Dewey's (1897) belief that a teacher's starting point should focus on establishing the child's interests and passions.

TWO STRANDS OF EDUCATION

Very broadly speaking, two strands of educational philosophy have been evidenced in schooling since the 19th century. The first suggests that education's purpose is to prepare students for life after school. As explained in Chapter 3, the neo-liberal approach, for example, would argue that education needs to prepare students to compete in a capitalist marketplace. The second strand, which is strongly linked to the progressive education movement in the early 1900s, contends that the starting point for education should be through addressing current, real-life issues. It is through this kind of active engagement that students develop the skills to face increasingly complex and demanding challenges over their lifetimes.

American educational philosopher, John Dewey, had much to say about authentic learning contexts, although he did not label them as such. For him, anything that was to be studied by children in schools "must be derived from the scope of ordinary life-experience" (Dewey, 1938/1997, p. 73). He was against learning abstract concepts and acquiring facts, simply because they might be useful in the future. Dewey's contemporary, Alfred North Whitehead (1929), highlighted the danger of teaching 'inert' knowledge that had little application or relevance to students' immediate lives. This kind of preparation for the future was, Dewey argued, "a treacherous idea" (p. 47). For Dewey, an educational task that does not originate in an actual situation is to "start on a course of dead work" or "busy work" (p. 112). Education needs to involve students directly engaging with real-world issues; after all, isn't that what students will be expected to do once they leave school?

At the root of Dewey's (1916/2004) educational beliefs was the notion that the underlying fundamental purpose of education was to prepare students to be active citizens in a democratic society. This kind of preparation for future experiences was, however, solidly rooted in 'present life'. Indeed, he believed that education was a "process of living and not a preparation for future living" (Dewey, 1897, p. 7).

This statement is of central importance to this chapter's (and indeed the book's) argument that education needs to be located in a student's everyday world—among the issues that are faced by people each and every day. Many facts or items of knowledge have little to no inherent value; their value derives from relationships to other things. Seen this way, an education that is not intertwined with learners' real lives is "a poor substitute for the genuine reality and tends to cramp and to deaden" (Dewey, 1897, p. 7). It is remarkable to see an educator, writing more than a hundred years ago, be such a fervent critic of traditional education and be so attuned to what useful and engaging education can look like.

We'll continue with Dewey just a little longer, since he did have two more key concepts that support our notion of authenticity. These are *interaction* and *continuity* (1938/1997). While Dewey worked at the University of Chicago, his work was heavily aligned with what was called the 'Chicago School' of sociology. This brand of sociology was concerned with how humans construct meaning about the world around them through their interactions with physical, abstract and social objects (see, for example, Blumer, 1969). From an 'interactionist' perspective, the role of the teacher is to decide upon which settings will afford learners opportunities to interact with rich and stimulating objects. Seen this way, the teacher is not defining the learning outcomes, but is choosing stimulating settings within which learners can create personally relevant meanings through their interactions.

Continuity, the second of Dewey's (1938/1997) concepts that is helpful in this section, posits the notion that educationally worthwhile experiences must build on past experiences and lead to fruitful future experiences. Dewey claims that "every experience both takes up something from those which have gone before and modifies in some way the quality of those which come after" (p. 35). This in itself may not seem particularly earth-shattering; this principle, however, becomes more useful as an analytic tool if we recall that it is a spectrum. Every kind of education, from learning Latin verbs by rote to writing letters to politicians, possesses a degree of continuity from what happened before to what might unfold later. Educators, Dewey argued, need to concern themselves with ensuring that students are engaged in activities that provide a high level of continuity. Other academics, such as Boud, Cohen and Walker (1993), draw from Dewey's principles when claiming that "unless new ideas and new experiences link to previous experience, they exist as abstractions, isolated and without meaning" (p. 8). Meaningful learning experiences cannot "exist in a vacuum that is independent of other experiences" (Beames, Higgins & Nichol, 2011, p. 12). Learning through experience is inextricably linked to what happened before and what may come to pass in the future.

The key question that Dewey implored teachers to ask themselves is as relevant today as it was in 1938:

Does this form of growth create conditions for further growth?

(p. 36)

53

Dewey (1938/1997) argued that the merit of any given experience could be judged by the "ground of what it moves toward and into" (p. 38). Teachers, then, need to be able to make judgments about how their practices can shape the learner's current direction, by recognizing the "attitudes and habitual tendencies" that are being created (p. 39). Doing this well demands that teachers must have a deep understanding of their students, in order to have a clear picture of "what is actually going on in the minds of those who are learning" (p. 39). The quality of the experience and the cognitive and affective state of the learner need to be carefully overseen by the educator. Just because the education is taking place in an authentic learning context does not mean that the learner is on their own or that the level of academic engagement needs to be any lower than it might be in the classroom. On the contrary, it is quite possible that the level of highly focused academic involvement might increase for some students once they begin interacting with real-world issues.

CONTEXTUALIZED LEARNING

At the heart of authenticity and education is learning in real-world contexts. Contextualized learning, or contextualization, is a term that is frequently heard in educational circles, and rightly so, as it implies a certain engagement of the educational activity with what is going on around it, what has happened before and what happens afterwards (rather like Dewey's continuity). Contextualized educational approaches 'locate' the learner and the content to be learned within a greater whole: neither is isolated or unrelated to the world around them. Central to this approach is a process that integrates "academic content with situations or issues that are meaningful to students" (Imel, 2000, p. 1), and which "goes far beyond drill-oriented, stimulus-and-response methodologies" (Centre for Occupational Research & Development, n.d., para. 4).

Hull and Souders (1996) explain that learning can be enhanced as students make sense of new information in relation to their 'frame of reference', which comprises their own memories and experiences. It is crucial to meaningful learning that students do not see various subjects, and the assessment tasks within them, as "hoops that need to be jumped through" as "the price of admission to the real event" of life and living (Dirkx, Amey & Haston, 1999, p. 102). As Nelsen and Seaman (2011) succinctly put it, "context matters" (p. 567). Too often, they argue, there seems to be a philosophical disconnection between the kind of learning that is personally relevant to students (since it is useful to them outside of school) and how judgments about students' intelligence are made using universalized and decontextualized tools of inquiry.

This chapter's principal argument is that many 'real-world' educational settings offer highly meaningful opportunities to learn curriculum in contexts that are authentic, as they take place in the school grounds, local neighbourhoods, and in conjunction with local businesses and institutions. We are fully aware that teaching in what some might call 'the real world' can mean a lot more work for the teacher, as it is rarely the same, and almost never follows a linear path. However, there is growing evidence that teaching in authentic settings can considerably increase the level of student engagement, as they begin to see how the concepts they are learning can be put to use in real-world contexts (Imel, 2000). This has several potential knock-on effects, too, such as fewer discipline issues, since learners are less likely to be bored or disinterested.

It is worth highlighting that incorporating real-world learning contexts into our teaching does not mean that all of the teaching and learning takes place outside the classroom. On the contrary, much may still take place indoors, as these are the 'home bases' where students have access to resources and information technology, and where they may be able to more deeply concentrate and study on their chosen project.

It is easy to see how ideas of contextualized learning are based in a constructivist paradigm. Constructivism, in essence, contends that people construct knowledge about the world through their interactions in it (see, for example, Vygotsky, 1978). Seen this way, the meanings that we ascribe to given objects, people and feelings are "not universal or independent of either the situation or the knower" (Dirkx et al., 1999, p. 99). Knowledge is not some grand and fixed thing that is 'out there', waiting for learners to discover; knowledge is something that we construct through our interactions (Blumer, 1969). This idea may seem simple enough, but it lies in contrast to "traditional notions of technical-rational knowledge" that has driven educational policy and practice for decades (Dirkx et al., 1999, p. 100). In educational terms, this constructivist-inspired, context-sensitive view places principal importance on the meanings that are constructed by the students, rather than on those driven by the teacher (Mahoney, 1991). Central to constructivism is the tenet that student learning needs to start within the concrete worlds with which they are most familiar (Brown, 2008). Brown's statement contests much accepted adventure-based education literature, which quite deliberately removes participants from the worlds they know best.

TRANSFERRING LEARNING BETWEEN CONTEXTS

If an educational programme removes learners from the worlds they inhabit, takes them to unfamiliar surroundings and engages them in novel activities, then efforts must be made to connect learning 'back to' everyday life—otherwise the educational value of such enterprises is highly questionable. As discussed in Chapter 4, the idea of transfer of learning has been a foundational concept in adventure education since the 1980s (see, for example, Gass, 1985; Priest & Gass, 1997). The central assumption is that learning that happens in one context can be transferred to another. In these adventure programmes, it is the intra- and inter-personal skills that are supposed to be transferrable between contexts. So, if one learns communication skills or gains self-confidence in one context (e.g., a two-day challenge course programme), then one can apply this learning in other contexts (e.g., at the home, office or school)—or so the argument goes. The argument also contends that this transfer can be 'metaphoric', because the activities are chosen to replicate the structure of certain challenges encountered in real life (e.g., getting the entire group over the 12-foot-high wall being used as a metaphor for the challenges of undertaking a big project at the office). Programmes such as a two-day challenge course remain popular in some parts of the world, despite the increased criticism that they have received concerning their limited capacity to elicit enduring transferrable learning (e.g., Brookes 2003a, 2003b; Brown, 2010).

There are two fundamental differences between the above kind of educational programme and what can be considered to be authentic. First, there is little in the way of an authentic context. How does an exercise that involves building a raft out of bamboo, barrels and ropes help a person learn about the world around them or make society a better place? It would be very difficult to demonstrate such an outcome, as the exercise is predicated on the tenuous assumption that behaviours demonstrated in one setting will be replicated in another, very different one.

The second big difference between much adventure education practice and learning in authentic contexts is that, with the latter, the intended learning outcomes relate to both content and process. In a math, geography, science or history class, the content can be purposefully connected to the lives of the learners. For example, in history, students might investigate how and why a street got its name as a means of looking at issues such as immigration, the commemoration of a battle or a 'heroic' figure. In adventure education, the teaching of content (e.g., skills of fire lighting or learning about the migratory patterns of the arctic tern) is often marginalized through lack of time and the prioritization of the development of personal and social skills (e.g., self-confidence, leadership or team work). Let us be clear though: adventure educators do not have a monopoly on this kind of intra- and inter-personal development. We have seen chemistry teachers (working entirely indoors) who appear to be far more capable at fostering young people's personal and social development than many outdoor instructors.

Our main point in this section is that authentic education approaches do not require learning to be transferred from one setting to a very different one, such as being courageous on a ropes course to being courageous when public speaking. If learning takes place in real contexts that are deeply intertwined with a child's real life, there is little need to transfer what is learned. What is learned will have direct relevance and be readily applicable.

PLACE-RESPONSIVE AND COMMUNITY-BASED EDUCATION

Our discussions about authentic learning contexts are inseparable from discourses on place-based, or place-responsive learning. Succinctly put, place-based education is about exploring a place's inherent curriculum. After all, everywhere, to some degree, has math, geography, history, science and art within it. Anywhere can be thought about, written about, discussed and even transformed—for better or for worse. By having students engage with a place's inherent curriculum, that place is no longer 'anywhere'; it becomes a 'storied' place that is full of meaning for those who have sought to become part of it (Henderson, 2010). Indeed, teachers need to be careful to ensure that the places in which they are learning and the meanings ascribed to the phenomena unfolding within it have strong relevance to students' lives (Dirkx et al., 1999).

Wattchow and Brown (2011) suggested the following four key questions for place-responsive educators:

- What is here in this place?
- What will this place permit us to do?
- What will this place help us to do?
- How is this place interconnected with my home place?

To this list, we have added an additional question: *What can we learn here?*

Place-responsive education has gained traction since the 1990s, largely in response to the features of late modernity that we explored in Chapter 3. As discussed earlier, the conditions of late modernity may limit our capacity to "respect and care for the local places we call home and the remote places we encounter when we travel" (Wattchow & Brown, 2011, p. 51). Place-responsive education incorporates the local and its relationship to places further afield, urban and rural; it considers the past/present/future; can be implemented across the curriculum; encompasses interactions between land, humans, ecology; and involves aspects of dwelling, moving and responding to the particularities of places.

Gruenewald (2003), drawing on work by Freire (1970/1993) and Giroux (1988), highlights the need for what he calls a "critical pedagogy of place". This kind of education supports the questioning of inequalities of power and opportunity, encourages places to become understood at a much deeper level, and focuses on people transforming their places. For Gruenewald, the key outcome of place-responsive education is to enable human beings to live well in their places—both socially and ecologically.

Earlier in this chapter, we referred to community service projects as one of many types of real-world settings and issues in which students can get involved. In keeping with the accepted wisdom on place-responsive education (e.g., Gruenewald, 2003; Smith & Sobel, 2010; Wattchow & Brown, 2011), our view is that students should be given opportunities to be involved in some kind of educational enterprise that enables them to learn more about the place in which they live. Exemplary approaches might include their projects having an element of community enhancement or improvement (see, for example, Sobel, 2005; Smith & Sobel, 2010).

These two steps (knowing place and improving place) are important to highlight, as authentic learning doesn't necessarily need to include either. For example, it is possible that two students could learn about how to make money in the real world, by stealing from vulnerable, elderly people. Since education is essentially a moral enterprise (see, for example, Buzzelli & Johnston, 2001; Claxton, 2012), authentic approaches to learning need to be ethically supportable. This position finds support in Aristotelian philosophy that espouses developing moral and intellectual excellence through practice (see Hunt, 1991; Stonehouse, 2010; Stonehouse, Allison & Carr, 2011). Meaningful education for citizenship can best prepare young people for the future by having them engage with the pressing problems that they are faced with, in their schools and neighbourhoods and beyond, over a sustained period of time.

Strongly linked to place-responsive education is community-based education, which we have alluded to above. Although both of us have written about these topics elsewhere, there is so much inherent overlap between community- and place-based education and authentic learning contexts, that some of the arguments for their adoption bear repeating. In community-based education the crucial underlying assumption is that students' "own communities, whether rich or poor, provide a natural context for learning that matters to children" (Melaville, Berg & Blank, 2006, p. 11). The community, then, becomes reframed as authentic curriculum, where all subject areas exist in their purest form. Directly linking academic curriculum to local community phenomena removes "the artificial separation between the classroom and the real world", and has been shown to improve student academic outcomes (Blank & Berg, 2006, p. 8).

IMPLICATIONS FOR PRACTICE

How can our classes, courses and programmes be more authentic? The most straightforward answer to this question lies in basing students' learning within the curriculum that exists within the places that they live and go to school. Students and teachers—whether in a thriving metropolis or a secluded lake in the midst of a boreal forest—need to ask themselves, *What can we learn here?* Concrete, real-world phenomena are those that capture the minds of young people.

Of course, spending an afternoon building a raft with bamboo poles, rope and barrels can be fun, and learning how to find the prime factors of 706 may test one's mathematical skills, but unless there is very clever contextualization, students will not make links from either task to previous experiences and possible future ones.

Smith (2002) has done much work in the area of place- and community-based education and coined the term, "real world problem-solving". This approach involves students identifying "school or community issues that they would like to investigate and address" (p. 589). The young people then analyze the issues, devise solutions and take concrete steps to improve the identified issue. The teacher's role becomes one of facilitator; they make links between the problem and the official curriculum, help with finding resources and act as project advisor. This problem-based approach involves students taking a greater stake in their places. It is regarded as "both a pedagogy and a philosophy that links classrooms with communities and textbooks with the 'real world'" (Butin, 2010, p. xiv).

Following Smith and Sobel (2010), community-based learning can include focusing on local culture, nature, service and enterprise (see Beames et al., 2011).

As with the other dimensions of adventurous learning (e.g., Agency and Uncertainty), it is not a matter of educational experiences possessing or not possessing these features: these concepts exist on a spectrum, where at one end there are real-world learning contexts that feature students developing lifelong skills, and at the other end of the spectrum are activities that are highly contrived and have little relevance to day-to-day life. Of course, all education is to a certain degree contrived, but that discussion is for another book.

Central to this theme of authenticity—particularly to those using traditional adventure-based activities (e.g., ropes courses, climbing, expeditions)—is that the concept of 'transfer of learning' becomes embedded or natural, rather than being metaphoric. Learning in authentic settings does not need to be 'isomorphically framed' (see Priest & Gass, 1997), so that it can be applied in the real world; the learning is already happening in the real world.

As we will do in each of the next three chapters, we now invite you to consider the last two or three sessions that you've taught. Depending on the kind of educator you are, this might have been instructing an introduction to canoeing lesson or teaching a poetry class. If you put authenticity on a dimension, with highly authentic at one end and not very authentic at the other, where would you place your sessions? Now consider what small, feasible steps you can take to increase its level of authenticity.

SUMMARY

Education that is rooted in the phenomena of 'where students are' recognizes that places have an inherent curriculum, and is likely to enhance opportunities for authentic ways of learning. Like so many educational concepts, there is not one 'single bullet' to guide our teaching, but a number of overlapping, inter-related themes.

One of the key themes in this chapter is that students need to be able to link their educational classes and courses to past and future experiences. This can be achieved by contextualizing the learning in environments that students may encounter outside of school, through the course of their daily lives. If learning contexts are too far removed from these daily experiences, then students might have difficulty in seeing the relevance and applicability that learning in a decontextualized setting might afford them. There is a growing body of literature suggesting that learning that occurs in local places has a high degree of meaning for participants (Brown, 2012a; Smith, 2002; Tooth & Renshaw, 2009).

Although we are obviously strong proponents of learning through authentic contexts, it needs to be stated that just because an educational site is located in the real world (e.g., a shopping mall or a local park) or the educational activity is focusing on a real-world issue (e.g., access to water in sub-Saharan Africa), does not mean that all students will automatically be responsive to that place. Much depends on the teacher, of course. Ultimately, the teacher's chief concern is to assist students as they identify and develop their own view of what "calls to be thought" in given real-world situations, and to "give the space for this to occur" (Bonnett & Cuyper, 2002, p. 339).

As we saw in Chapter 1, an educator is necessary for any learning to be labelled 'education'. We have seen wonderful, gifted teachers who are working entirely indoors and with little real-world context, and who teach ancient Greek history through assisting learners to make connections to modern democratic processes. By contrast, we have seen outdoor educators fool themselves into thinking they were demonstrating enlightened, best practices, yet were taking away choice and power from students, while completely ignoring local phenomena—the land's inherent curriculum.

Following Dewey (1938/1997), the contention that 'genuine education' comes from experience does not mean that all experiences have the same capacity to elicit learning. It is the teacher's role to manage these experiences in a way that ensures they are not "mis-educative"; and mis-educative experiences are, according to Dewey, those which stop "growth of further experience" (p. 25). The quality of the experience was a key issue for Dewey. Our main point in this chapter has been to argue that it is not enough for a teacher to teach in an outdoor setting or to have the class tackle a real-world issue; the way that this is done is also of central importance if learning is to be authentic.

Chapter 6
Agency and Responsibility

Many people who have observed a group of youngsters building a raft, or supporting each other on a challenge ropes course, may have been impressed by the general level of enthusiasm and busy-ness exhibited. These types of activities are often held up as examples of team building and leadership development. These may be some of the outcomes of participation—but they may not be. For example, some students might act as leaders, but some may also be silenced or ignored. Too often there is a haphazard or 'chance' aspect to this kind of learning or, more unfortunately, some students might have a mis-educative experience (Dewey, 1938/1997) that will put them off further involvement.

While it is clear that we view learning as a complex and messy affair that is far from a linear process, we believe it is important to provide adventurous learning experiences which offer opportunities for students to enhance or develop capacities that will open new doors, stimulate questions and assist them in reaching their potential. Thus, we consider it important to think carefully about what it is we might want to achieve through participation in adventurous learning.

In this chapter we will:

- Highlight the value of agency and autonomy in fostering learning.
- Discuss the importance of facilitating appropriate choices for students in order to encourage engagement and learning.
- Emphasize the importance for learners to take ownership and have responsibility for their learning.

A central theme in this chapter is how educators can support the development of student autonomy. This can be achieved through providing opportunities for students to be responsible for their learning as they plan and undertake meaningful adventure experiences. We realize that 'meaningful' is a loaded term that differs across different age groups and cultural contexts. So, we are intentionally non-prescriptive in how we define meaningful. Meaningfulness is contingent upon learners' needs, rather than on the blanket application of a fixed educational script.

The literature of adventure education is replete with calls for active participation and choice, and there are many 'how-to' books that provide fun games and activities. However, as we alluded to in Chapter 4, how activities are delivered has a large bearing on what it is that students experience and learn. The development of agency and autonomy, and the ability to take responsibility for one's actions, is not as simple as participating in a challenge ropes course or rappelling off a 20-metre cliff. As with many aspects of teaching and learning, the obvious solution is not always the most appropriate one. We have argued that the effects of rationalization and the commodification of adventure experiences frequently serve to position the learner as consumer. The ability to display agency and develop autonomy is limited in highly regulated adventure activities, with the justifiable need to conform to safety requirements in sessions involving height, steep ground or moving water. In the sections that follow, we build a case for the value of students exercising agency and developing autonomy, and the value of linking actions to responsibility.

AGENCY

Learner agency is important, for as we understand more about the complexities of learning involving the social, cultural and physical worlds of the learner, it is helpful to consider the opportunities for active participation (Mercer, 2011). Agency has been defined as "the capability of individual human beings to make choices and to act on these choices in ways that make a difference in their lives" (Martin 2004, p. 135). Agency is often discussed in connection with the term 'structure'—hence the classic 'structure versus agency' debates in the sociology literature. Structure refers to the contextual features (e.g., institutions, social relations, policies) in which individuals find themselves. One line of argument is that agency is restricted due to powerful forces (structures) that inhibit individual choice and action. The counter-position is that as agents we are able to be self-determining individuals with the ability to shape our own worlds. A third position, which advocates for a more balanced perspective, acknowledges that both the individual and the context interact in "a relationship of reciprocal causality" (Mercer, 2011, p. 428). We adopt this middle ground and acknowledge that we are influenced by the context—but we are also in a position to change that context (to greater or lesser degrees).

As we argue throughout the book, we can bring about change by both shifting the emphasis on the context (rethinking what adventurous activities are) and by helping learners to develop greater autonomy in order to be agents of change. We do not just react to our surroundings, controlled by an unseen puppeteer; we have the potential to resist and to be creative. Dearden (1972) explains that people are autonomous when their thoughts and actions come from within, rather than being driven by what someone else tells them do or what the media tells them to think. Whatever a person thinks and acts is directly connected to her own "choices, deliberations, decisions, reflections, judgements, plannings or reasonings" (p. 453).

It has been suggested that effective and motivated learners are those who see themselves as having agency to shape their learning experiences (Mercer, 2011). One way that agency has been fostered in educational settings is through a focus on providing opportunities for learners to develop autonomy.

DEVELOPING LEARNER AUTONOMY

In an educational setting, autonomy refers to a learner's ability to take self-determined action based on intrinsic motivation, rather than being a passive agent of external forces (e.g., merely following instructions). Autonomy has been defined as the ability to choose one's course of action and to be responsible for this choice (Deci & Ryan, 1987). The premise is that a learner who is intrinsically motivated will act because they are interested in an activity and enjoy it for its own sake, rather than for an external reward.

The benefits of learner autonomy find strong support in both education literature (Black & Deci, 2000; Reeve, 2002; Stefanou, Perencevich, DiCintio & Turner, 2004) and adventure education (Sibthorp, Paisley & Gookin, 2007; Sibthorp, Paisley, Gookin & Furman, 2008). Sibthorp and colleagues (2008) found that many studies have successfully demonstrated that teachers who support student autonomy "are more effective at fostering both academic and developmental outcomes including perceived competence, self-esteem, creativity, and conceptual understanding" (p. 137).

Similarly, Grolnick, Ryan and Deci (1991) reported that learners who felt supported in their efforts to be autonomous had positive experiences towards tasks, were more engaged and were more likely to value their own involvement in the activity. Rather than focusing on motivating their students through external pressure, educators who encourage autonomy will display empathy for the learners' perspectives by enabling them to make choices, take initiative, and solve their own problems. Bohlin, Durwin and Reese-Weber (2012) report that students of autonomy supportive educators show signs of being engaged in deep, meaningful learning; being more creative; obtaining higher levels of achievement; and experiencing enhanced well-being.

Much of the work on autonomy is based on self-determination theory (Deci & Ryan, 1987; Ryan & Deci, 2000). Self-determination theory (SDT) posits that people have innate needs for autonomy, competence, and relatedness. The theory draws attention to the value of *autonomy* in the regulation of intentional behaviour. The theory also stresses people's desire to feel *competent* and to experience mastery. The final component, *relatedness*, refers to the sense of feeling connected to others so that we feel safe and secure. This sense of relatedness provides an environment that is conducive to exploration and experimentation with new ideas and courses of action.

More recent empirical research from the learning outside the classroom sector has drawn on SDT theory to shown that "less self-regulated pupils profit more from the outdoor setting than those who show already a high intrinsic learning regulation" (Dettweiler et al., 2015, p. 12). The outdoor science lab that this work refers to indicated that this kind of adventurous learning appeals to students who are less motivated by conventional, didactic classroom approaches.

There are some connections or intersections between aspects of self-determination theory and Bandura's (1977, 1982) description of the role of self-efficacy in human agency. Self-efficacy refers to an individual's perception of their capability to achieve success in a particular area of activity. Bandura (1982) pointed out that it is difficult to change behaviours by will power alone; rather, learners need opportunities to exercise agency and gain mastery of skills. He went on to argue that the "inability to influence events and social conditions that significantly affect one's life can give rise to feelings of futility and despondency as well as anxiety" (p. 140). Therefore, in order for learners to effectively enhance their sense of self-efficacy on any given task, it is vitally important for them to be given opportunities to make meaningful choices that are free from external pressures. The opportunity to gain a sense of mastery, which leads to developments in self-efficacy, requires a shift in the types of activity that might be offered as part of an adventure education programme. We will discuss the role of mastery in adventurous learning in greater detail in Chapter 8.

THE ROLE OF CHOICE

In addition to the change in focus from participation to mastery comes a necessary shift in the relationships between the learner and teacher/educator/instructor. If learners are to have opportunities to exercise choice and autonomy, then those who have traditionally been in 'charge' of the provision of will need to relinquish some of their power and influence over learners (Bandura, 1982). This shift in relationships between the learner and the educator, in order to develop learner autonomy, has its roots in self-determination theory's notion of autonomy support. *Autonomy support*, alluded to above, refers to the educator taking the learner's perspective into account by devising learning tasks that have relevance, acknowledging the learner's feelings and supplying positive feedback on competence, and by fostering opportunities for choice while minimizing external pressures (Sibthorp et al., 2008; Stefanou et al., 2004).

Implementing appropriate teaching strategies to support the development of autonomy is not necessarily as simple as just providing students with choice; choices that are offered must have meaning and need to be associated with consequences and intended learning outcomes. Stefanou et al. (2004) note that autonomy support is too often simply equated with giving students choice which can be meaningless, and ends up actually undermining student engagement with learning (e.g., choosing between cooking a meal and washing up).

The principles underpinning autonomy support provide a useful framework for us to think about how we might implement adventurous learning experiences in order to maximize opportunities for students to exercise and learn autonomy. Our attention will now turn to the types of choice that we might offer learners.

AUTONOMY SUPPORT

Stefanou et al. (2004) defined three types of choices that are offered to students to foster autonomy: organizational, procedural and cognitive.

Organizational autonomy support encourages student 'ownership of the environment'. This might include the teacher offering students opportunities to develop 'group rules', make choices over the rate of progress toward a goal, and set dates for submission of assignments. *Procedural autonomy support* encourages student 'ownership of form' and can include the teacher offering students a choice of media through which to present learning—for instance, making a video clip or an interactive display to illustrate a principle of economics. *Cognitive autonomy support* encourages student 'ownership of learning' and can feature teachers asking students to argue their point, generate their own solution paths, and evaluate their own and others' ideas. Stefanou and colleagues (2004) suggest that "it is cognitive autonomy support that truly leads to the psychological investment in learning that so many educators strive for" (p. 101).

For clarity, we have combined organizational and procedural autonomy support under the label of *setting*. In adventure education practice we can see how learners have input into how the setting is constructed. Learners may be offered choices by establishing of a group contract that outlines acceptable behaviour; developing a roster for duties; and selecting activities (e.g., "today is a 'water day'—as a group you can choose to go rafting, canoeing, tubing or canyoning"). Learners might choose a leader of the day or they might be able to decide whether the end of an activity facilitation session will take the form of drama, song, art or discussion. These are all examples of how a setting is established based on learner input and choice.

Learners need to be given choices and the questions we would ask are, *What freedom do they really have?* (e.g., when the choice is limited to a or b), *How do these types of choice engage the students at a deeper level?* (e.g., emotionally and cognitively) and *What is the connection between these choices, relevance to students' lives, and opportunities for taking responsibility?*

Stefanou et al. (2004) found that instances of organizational and procedural autonomy support were also prevalent in classrooms, such as when choosing a partner to work with or the presentational style of a project. They found cognitive autonomy support evident in situations where the teacher created the opportunities for students to initiate their own academic goals, to understand and be able to explain their thinking or pathway to finding a solution, or employing multiple approaches to dealing with a task. Sibthorp et al. (2008) have suggested that teachers adopt the following actions: ask for students' opinions, listening to answers, allow other students to contribute to the discussion, encourage effort and praise progress.

We hope you'll agree that there is a strong imperative for educators to be mindful of the types of choices they present to learners, and to move beyond simplistic choices relating to just the setting. Approaches that rely on choices of organization and procedure may not be powerful enough to enhance learners' levels of motivation and achievement (Assor, Kaplan & Roth, 2002; Stefanou et al., 2004). In fact, Stefanou et al. (2004) found that providing choice about learning tasks "had little impact on student perceptions of autonomy or on self-reported behaviors and cognitive engagement" (p. 100). So, when it comes to offering choices, what is needed are approaches to teaching that offer learners opportunities to exercise cognitive choices. This is not to immediately dismiss choices related to the setting. Rather, it is to acknowledge that choices may be necessary, but they are not in themselves "sufficient conditions for deep-level student engagement in learning" (p. 100).

Following Patrick Geddes, engaging students holistically (hand, head, heart) has become one of the hallmarks of good adventure education (Higgins & Nicol, 2010). Perhaps one of the greatest challenges for educators is to embed the 'head' (cognitive) component into a programme. From personal experience we know how adventure programmes are frequently positioned as an alternative to 'mainstream' schooling and an emphasis is often placed on learning-by-doing, rather than learning through reading or listening. One of the challenges laid down by an examination of the literature on choice and autonomy surrounds how might we provide experiences and support to enhance the development of learners' cognitive autonomy. As we saw in the previous chapter, one possible route to connecting with learners in the cognitive realm is through engaging them in authentic learning experiences that have direct relevance to their lives.

THE IMPORTANCE OF RELEVANCE AND INDEPENDENT THINKING

The issue of relevance, as an influence on the development of autonomy, was the focus of Assor and colleagues' (2002) study of over 850 school students. The opening phrase of the title of their paper *Choice is good, but relevance is excellent*, strongly hints at the important role that relevance has for enhancing learner autonomy. While the provision of choice is helpful, it "should not always be viewed as a major indicator of autonomy support" (Assor et al., 2002, p. 261). Based on student responses, the researchers identified the following autonomy-enhancing teacher behaviours: fostering relevance, providing choice and allowing criticism and encouraging independent thinking. Since the element of choice has been discussed above, we will focus on aspects of relevance and on encouraging criticism and independent thinking.

Relevance has been referred to as a task that is meaningful in some substantive way (Sibthorp et al., 2008). Fostering relevance involves teachers helping learners to "experience the learning process as relevant to and supportive of their self-determined interests, goals and values" (Assor et al., 2002, p. 264). Teachers explained how the educational tasks were related to the learner's personal goals and displaying empathy helped them gain a greater understanding of the task from the learner's perspective (Assor et al., 2002). Fostering relevance requires teachers to take an 'empathetic-active' role, which requires them to first understand learners' goals, interests and needs, and then link learning tasks to those goals, interests and needs.

Part of the empathetic-active role includes providing useful feedback to learners. Stefanou et al. (2004) highlight how providing learners with positive feedback about their levels of competence has also been identified as a useful strategy for supporting the development of responsibility and persistence. Viewed this way, the educator can play a vital role in the learning process and in the development of learner autonomy. Assor et al. (2002) also emphasize the active role that the educator needs to play. It is not sufficient for the educator to simply 'step back' and let learners discover things for themselves. The empathetic-active role requires purposeful engagement from the teacher, so that learners can work towards goals that are important to them. In Assor et al.'s study, fostering relevance, and aligning the learner's actions with their goals, interests or values, was a more important component of autonomy support than providing learners with choice.

The last of Assor et al.'s (2002) autonomy-enhancing teacher behaviour is allowing criticism and encouraging independent thinking. Their findings demonstrated that learners who were able to express dissatisfaction with a given task and who felt that the teacher might respond by modifying the task, experienced feelings of greater autonomy. Even if the teacher was unable to change the task, the act of addressing the learner's concerns and providing additional information about the rationale for the task helped the learner. This is perhaps one of the more challenging and potentially confronting issues faced by an educator. No one likes to think that their lesson plan or schedule of activities for the day will not meet with approval. The ability to acknowledge a disconnection between a 'well intentioned' plan and student response takes maturity, humility and a willingness to be flexible.

We are aware that we have not directly addressed teacher agency in any depth. Like the students they work alongside, teachers are also subjected to restrictions and opportunities that influence their practice. The most obvious of these include the rigidity of standardized testing and the prescribed curriculums that serve to limit teachers' capacities to teach in ways that champion student agency. Beyond these fixed elements, educators will have their own unique set of cultural, political and geo-physical circumstances that constrain and enable the ways in which they can teach. The four dimensions of adventurous learning can be seen as opportunities for teachers to exercise their own agency, as they strive to improve their students' learning and well-being.

A WORD OF CAUTION ABOUT TOO MUCH CHOICE

Although offering students choices is important, too many choices can be bewildering. Stefanou et al. (2004) advise limiting choice particularly with regard to those relating to what they call the setting. Examples of offering poor choices, might be something like "which group do you want to be in?" or "which initiative activity do you want to try first?" These choices can cause unnecessary confusion and lead to a failure to engage in deeper issues, such as students being given space to explain why they chose a particular course of action. Stefanou and colleagues explain that, "although choice and decision making are fundamental, more than simple choices about tasks or roles are necessary to influence students' decisions to become cognitively engaged in academic tasks" (p. 109). They contend that cognitive autonomy support is the key ingredient to learner motivation and engagement.

The importance of the educator's role, in terms of choosing learning activities that provide appropriate opportunities to exercise autonomy, cannot be over-stated. This is reflected in Sibthorp et al.'s (2008) comment that,

> if a leader is too open-ended with student options and must decline some of the student choices, students may feel that the leader has reneged on a promise and will likely undermine the leader's efforts at

autonomy support. Staff must walk a fine line between offering realistic decisions to students that do not jeopardize safety yet are meaningful in some significant way.

(p. 146)

This observation is pertinent as students are generally highly attuned to a session's authenticity (see Chapter 5), and will quickly work out when they are given a low-stake, 'pseudo-choice' of little consequence. They will very readily come to an understanding of whether their choice really matters by the manner in which they are held accountable for the consequences of their decisions. Although often well intentioned, early intervention ('rescuing') serves to undermine attempts to build autonomy and to clearly connect choices and actions with outcomes. The teacher, parent or leader who either chooses to constantly intervene, or who is required to in order to keep the activity safe, is hindering the development of autonomous and responsible young people.

RESPONSIBILITY

Fraser (2008) has remarked that, "in order for students to engage deeply in learning, for their sake, not ours, they need opportunities for ownership and responsibility. When students own their learning and feel responsible for it we tap the most powerful reservoir of potential" (p. 9). As detailed above, providing learners with appropriate choices is one way for them to develop greater autonomy, be agents of their own learning and take ownership of the outcomes. When students are engaged in activities that have relevance to their lives, where they have meaningful choices, are provided with positive feedback on their competence, and can gain a sense of accomplishment (mastery), their intrinsic motivation increases and they are better placed to take responsibility for their learning.

Facilitating this requires teachers to think carefully about the types of responsibility they offer learners and what might result if they do not take this seriously. Giving students responsibility and then undermining that, or removing the consequences, sends them a clear message that they are not being trusted. We believe that it is important that the responsibility–consequence pairing should not be viewed as a negative—as in, if you don't do X, a terrible thing (Y) will happen. On the converse, we know that acting responsibly brings many favourable consequences, such as thorough preparation leading to a successful outdoor trip or stream restoration project.

Educational experiences should be designed so that learners can be held responsible for making meaningful choices, develop competence and see the connections between action and outcome. For example, Sibthorp et al. (2008) have emphasized how fostering perceptions of ownership and responsibility for adventure programmes impacted favourably on students' leadership and outdoor skills. Good educators will progressively sequence activities so that students will gain in competence and confidence, take responsibility for their actions, and have opportunities to reflect on the learning process (i.e., metacognition). It is not reasonable to ask learners to take responsibility for an outcome that either contained an element of luck, or that was determined without respect to the level of commitment displayed by the learner. Therefore, handing over responsibility to learners, or asking them to take responsibility for an outcome, should come with opportunities to exercise autonomy, display competence and see the relevance of the task to other aspects of their lives.

DISCUSSION

Clearly, agency, autonomy and responsibility are linked. Autonomy involves the opportunity to make choices and these choices are given meaning, in part, by the level of responsibility that the learner feels. If the consequences of a choice are removed, then what investment will a learner have in the endeavour? The deeper issues at play here relate to the types of choices (and the significance that they have for the learner) and the connection between choice and outcome for which the learner might have responsibility.

The types of choices that we offer need to be well thought out and should drive the activity on offer rather than the other way around. Too often adventure educators are limited in the type of choices and the levels of responsibility that they can make available to learners because of the inherent risks in many popular 'adventure' activities. While it might appear that we give choice on the challenge ropes course (e.g., "choose who you want to partner with" or "select three of the following eight activities"), these choices remain at the 'setting' level. Obviously, we can't let learners choose how to put a harness on or choose to use a belay device any way they wish, as the associated risks limits options.

Historically, adventure education placed importance on issues of choice and responsibility in the design of programmes. We are concerned, however, that somewhere along the way adventure has been equated with activities rather than with the often messy endeavour of learning, discovering and being engaged in uncertainty that is the real adventure of life. It's time to sharpen our focus on the needs of the learner, rather than the supposed adventure activity. Learning can be adventurous if we are prepared to be supportive of learners in their struggle to take responsibility for their learning and stop being 'guru-like' figures who believe the solutions lie in activities that, far from being adventurous, continue to position learners as passive recipients rather than as active autonomous actors.

Just as we did at the end of the Authenticity chapter (5), take a few moments to consider the last two sessions that you've taught—or that are typical of what and how you teach. Where would you place your session on the Agency dimension? How much room is there for your students to make meaningful choices and exercise autonomy? In what ways can you begin to increase the degree of student agency in your teaching?

SUMMARY

We suggest that many contemporary forms of adventure activities do not actually offer meaningful choices that involve students at a deeper level, nor do they offer them opportunities to take responsibility for their actions. This chapter has shown how the literature on youth development attests to the importance of agency, autonomy and responsibility in the development of young people. Importantly, developing autonomy requires thoughtful consideration of appropriate choices—both in terms of their quality and consequence and the amount. Finally, educators need to think carefully about the learning processes, that will foster autonomy, and shift their gaze from focusing primarily on activities that may restrict the development of autonomy and opportunities to be responsible for one's learning.

One particular strength that school teachers and teachers-in-training can bring to discussions about outdoor learning, is a comprehension of the primacy of the learner in programme design. Adventure educators—who increasingly appear to focus on selecting activities from a suite of offerings and then deciding what the learning outcomes might have been—have much to learn from school teachers. Educators who are attuned to their students' needs will understand young people's capacity to be agents of their own learning in a world where knowledge, technology and social arrangements are increasingly fluid in nature. Our attention now turns to the third dimension of adventurous learning: uncertainty.

Chapter 7

Uncertainty

Of the four elements of adventure that we discuss, the element of uncertainty represents a cornerstone of adventurous learning. We saw in Chapter 1 that many definitions of adventure invoke references to uncertainty of outcome. We wish to emphasize the oft neglected, but important point, that uncertainty in the *process* of educating provides many opportunities to enrich learning experiences and to engage students in unanticipated ways. When there is uncertainty, one is required to find new solutions and experiment with new ideas or actions; one has space to be creative rather than repeating previous actions. While developing creativity may seem like a necessary requirement for any engaging educational enterprise, administrative policies at state and national levels may constrain teachers' and students' freedom to blaze a personally relevant learning trail, rather than following a well-trodden, one-size-fits-all approach to gaining knowledge.

In this chapter we will:

- Discuss the meanings of uncertainty in education.
- Explain the value of creativity in learning and how it can be fostered.
- Explore three inter-related concepts: cognitive dissonance, assimilation and accommodation.
- Elaborate on the educational merits of developing uncertainty tolerance and uncertainty competence.
- Describe the principal ways in which teachers can more deliberately incorporate elements of uncertainty.

As discussed in Chapter 3, certain features of the time in which we live, such as neo-liberal market-force agendas, have led to business models driving educational practice. Rationalized, efficient systems thrive on controlling the process by which products are constructed and services are rendered. At international fast food chain restaurants, there is very little scope to deviate from the way the food is prepared or delivered or consumed. If the overall goals of education were to prepare young people to work within very tightly defined roles in globally homogeneous workplaces, then a fixed, universal system of educating and testing students might be desirable. As discussed earlier, critics have argued that many schools currently teach and test in these very prescribed and standard-ized ways.

In Chapter 3 we also discussed how late modern society is characterized by its liquidity (Bauman, 2007), mobility (Elliot, 2014) and uncertainty (Beck, 1992). It follows that we must educate young people in a manner that is aligned with the world around them. Education needs to give students the tools to live well in a world that is increasingly uncertain, and this needs to be done through approaches to teaching and learning that embrace uncertainty, and which equip learners not just to cope, but to thrive.

A HISTORY OF UNCERTAINTY AND EDUCATION

The notion of deliberately incorporating elements of uncertainty into teaching practices is not a new one. Aristotle (384–322 BC) claimed that practical wisdom—what he called phronesis—was gained from prac-tising reasoning and by making moral decisions (Stonehouse, 2010). A question that has only one right answer, such as 'What is the formula for the sine height method of measuring tree height?', does not require the kind of reasoning that Aristotle had in mind. A question like, 'How can we measure the height of this tree?', is one that requires the learner to investigate the various ways that can be used to perform this task. Naturally, we would hope that this problem would have been raised by the student in the investigation of a meaningful issue (e.g., situating a vegetable plot to maximize direct sunlight).

Fast-forward to the 20th century and we see that the pre-eminent thinker from the progressive education movement, John Dewey, also had some clear ideas regarding the kinds of learning tasks that students should encounter. Although being a somewhat impenetrable read, Dewey's book, *Logic: The Theory of Inquiry* (1938), makes an especially vital point

75

for educators to heed. Here, Dewey explained how "indeterminate situations"—those which aren't clearly defined and which don't have obvious resolutions—are central to effective learning. This is so because a situation's 'indeterminateness' is what will pique people's curiosity and motivate them to find solutions in order to make the situation 'determinate'. Indeed, Dewey viewed living itself as a perpetual rhythm between periods of disequilibrium, which demand some kind of resolution, and journeys towards equilibrium and harmony (Nelsen & Seaman, 2011).

Dewey counsels us to remember that all questions contain a need to know and an element of doubt. We embark on a quest to learn to resolve the need and remove the doubt (Garrison, 1999). Garrison explains how the American educational philosopher agreed with Aristotle that it was inquiry that permitted reflection and fostered in people the willingness and ability to deliberate and make intelligent choices.

In terms of how this relates to teaching and learning, the onus is on educators to provide our students with opportunities for intelligent deliberation which arises from them encountering indeterminate situations (i.e., uncertainty). Intelligent deliberation can be seen as a rigorous academic exercise that features "a tentative trying-out of various courses of action" (Dewey, 1922, p. 202). A short-hand way to say this might be 'developing creativity in solving problems'. When seen from this perspective, there is an educational imperative for teachers to ensure that their students find themselves at metaphorical 'forks in the road', which demand their reasoning and which will in turn inform what they do. Dewey's idea of practical reasoning includes both critical reflection and careful deliberation upon the possible consequences of various courses of action (Garrison, 1999). Reasoning, it should be remembered, is a mental exercise, where imaginary acts are not set in stone (Dewey, 1922).

Critical reflection, intelligent deliberation and practical reasoning are holistic, living and organic processes (Garrison, 1999, p. 301)—usually because complex issues in the real world demand such holistic and multi-faceted responses. Dewey argues that "education *through* occupations combines within itself more of the factors conducive to learning than any other method" (1916/2004, p. 297). Here, Dewey defines an occupation as "a continuous activity having purpose" (p. 297). We know that Dewey was not a proponent of vocational training to prepare people for jobs, so that's not the meaning of occupation he is employing here (see DeFalco, 2010). On the contrary, Dewey's (1915/1990) idea of education through occupations is founded on the assumption that growth "comes from the continual interplay of ideas and their embodiment in action" (p. 133). The end point for the student is not some instrumental gain or external badge; the educational value of a given activity is rooted in the uncertainty and indeterminateness of the situation.

CREATIVITY

Robinson (2011) advocates for education to more deliberately focus on cultivating children's "powers of creativity" (p. 5). He claims that despite the "sheer unpredictability of human affairs" (p. 5), children's capacities to be creative are being schooled out of them. The following quote summarizes the root of his critique:

> Current approaches to education and training are hobbled by assumptions about intelligence and creativity that have squandered the talents and stifled the creative confidence of untold numbers of people. This waste stems partly from an obsession with certain types of academic ability and from a preoccupation with standardized testing.
>
> (2011, p. 8)

Robinson (2011) explains how governments all over the world are investing heavily in educational reform that narrows the curriculum, emphasizes standardized testing and limits teachers' capacities to decide what to teach and how to teach it. The unfortunate irony lies in the way these forms serve to stifle "the very skills and qualities that are essential to meet the challenges we face: creativity, cultural understanding, communication, collaboration and problem solving" (p. 5). In this light, education is responsible for limiting our students' capacities to flourish in contemporary society. To be clear, Robinson's argument is based on the premises that, (1) the world is becoming increasingly unpredictable and moving at ever-increasing speeds, (2) organizations of all kinds require creative thinkers who can work well with others and who are highly adaptable, and (3) despite all of this, educational systems are not responding effectively to either issue.

Creativity, according to Robinson (2011), comprises three related elements. The first of these is imagination, "which is the process of bringing to mind things that are not present to our senses" (pp. 2–3). The second element is creativity itself, "which is the process of developing original ideas that have value" (p. 2). The third element of creativity is innovation, "which is the process of putting new ideas into practice" (p. 3). Robinson advocates for an initial stage of dreaming up all manner of possibilities, followed by subsequent stages of developing feasible ideas into useful action. Importantly, once ideas are generated, students need to decide which ones to pursue and then go through a period of testing and refining that demands critical thinking (Robinson, 2011).

Educational psychologist Eleanor Duckworth has written extensively about what she calls *the having of wonderful ideas*, which has strong resonance with our concepts of authenticity and how creativity is a part of responding to life's uncertainties. Duckworth (2011) explains that children need to be "afforded the occasions to be intellectually creative" (p. 12). These 'occasions' arise from educators providing settings that offer opportunities to come up with wonderful ideas that can help them address "intellectual problems that are real to them" (p. 7). For Duckworth, this element of intellectual engagement is far more important than anything decided beforehand regarding "what children *ought* to know" or "*ought* to be able to do at a certain age" (p. 3).

As with writers like Whitehead (1929), who expressed his disdain of the acquisition of 'inert ideas', Duckworth (2011) saw no point in education that focused primarily on gaining "a dry, contentless set of tools" (p. 13). In her view, once children had something 'real' to consider, the necessary tools could not help but develop.

Creativity guru, Robert Sternberg (2003), has outlined 24 different ways that teachers can foster this kind of creative thinking. We won't list all of them here, but two of them in particular have strong resonance with adventurous learning. The first is the importance of 'cross-fertilization' between subjects and disciplines. An example of this is how a student with an interest in cars might be encouraged to see them through engineering, historical, cultural, mathematical and environmental impact lenses. This point finds solid support in Dewey's (1938/1997) ideas of rooting learning in children's interests.

The second of Sternberg's (2003) keys to facilitating creative thinking that is especially important to adventurous learning is very simple: educators need to give students enough time to be creative. As explained in Chapter 3, late modern society demands that everything, from internet speed to pizza delivery, is done at an increasingly faster pace. Creativity, however, requires time—time to consider different courses of action, to make mistakes, to refine ideas and come up with solutions that have value.

The onus is once again placed on the educator, as they must allow students the space to think creatively, while ensuring that they encounter just enough uncertainty to require creative solutions, but not so much uncertainty and dissonance that they cannot cope.

COGNITIVE DISSONANCE, ASSIMILATION AND ACCOMMODATION

Current discussions surrounding uncertainty are, to an extent, derivatives of Festinger's early work on the theory of *cognitive dissonance* (1957) and Piaget's (1977, 1980) concepts of *assimilation* and *accommodation*. Cognitive dissonance theory outlines how people manage inconsistencies between their thoughts, actions and environment. People's inconsistent beliefs might be unrelated to each other (in which case there is no problem), or they may be related, and be either consonant (in agreement) or dissonant (contradictory). For example, I am a climber and I like Volkswagen cars—these two positions are unrelated. In contrast, I might be a climber and an environmentalist, in which case I might have trouble reconciling my carbon footprint from flying to Spain to go climbing. These actions can lead to feelings of dissonance or confusion that I might try and resolve through elaborate attempts to justify or minimize the consequences of my actions. Festinger's work explained how people try to minimize this dissonance by interpreting events in a manner that will "maintain consistency between their beliefs, actions and behaviours" (Brown, 2008, p. 7).

It has been argued in some adventure education textbooks that focusing on artificially creating situations that will elicit strong feelings of cognitive dissonance will lead to greater learning and growth (see, for example, Walsh & Golins, 1976; Priest & Gass, 1997). Drawing on psychological literature, however, Brown (2008) has explained how

> the premise that the active promotion of disequilibrium is necessary to promote learning is contestable. A situation which engenders disequilibrium may be treated by learners as too great a 'leap' in understanding and meaning in which case they might reject it outright or otherwise consign it to the 'not valid in the real world' file.
>
> (p. 7)

Closely related to cognitive dissonance theory are Piaget's (1977, 1980) classic psychological concepts of *assimilation* and *accommodation*.

79

Assimilation involves the integration of new and reasonably similar experiences into existing cognitive structures (McInerney & McInerney, 1998). If, however, the new experiences are indeed novel, then a person will have to modify an existing cognitive structure in order for the new experience to be incorporated. This process is called accommodation.

Festinger's (1957) work is helpful in showing educators how a certain amount of cognitive dissonance is needed in order to ensure that students are assimilating and accommodating new information—re-equilibrating, in a sense. However, if an 'educational' experience is so alien to a student's cognitive structure that she cannot understand it, it is possible that no learning will take place at all (Hergenhahn, 1982). So, rather than a new experience being accommodated into existing patterns of thought, it may be "dismissed as irrelevant or impossible" (Brown, 2008, p. 5).

Brown's (2008) critique of the 'comfort zone' model challenged the seemingly uncontested assumption that artificially increasing cognitive dissonance (aka disequilibrium) was a direct path to participant learning. Despite convincing arguments from the adventure therapy literature that personal growth is most likely to take place when people feel safe, secure and accepted (Davis-Berman & Berman, 2002), practices that involve making people feel uncomfortable (or scared) by presenting them with tasks that they perceive to be too challenging to overcome, continue to be used. This questionable practice is compounded when it is managed by instructors who have little or no training or qualification in therapy (Brown, 2008).

Following the discussion in the above section, the implication for educators is that students' tasks need to have just enough disequilibrium to arouse interest and present a challenge, while not being so over-whelming that they elicit protective emotional responses, and end up being more harmful than helpful. This idea is very closely linked to the key themes associated with mastery through challenge in Chapter 8.

Festinger and Piaget's psychological concepts are quite clearly con-nected to this chapter's focus on uncertainty. In educational contexts, some uncertainty and unpredictability is desirable, as it can arouse students' curiosity and motivate them to learn and encourage them to be creative, as they seek to find a solution or resolution to an issue. However, too much uncertainty can be counter-productive. As we will see in the next section, humans have individual tolerances for uncertainty, and it may be possible to teach students specific 'uncertainty competences' that can help them better deal with cognitive dissonance and become more skilled at accommodating new and unfamiliar experiences.

UNCERTAINTY TOLERANCE AND UNCERTAINTY COMPETENCES

Following on from our discussion in Chapter 3 about living in the 'liquid times' of late modernity, there is a related body of literature surrounding the 'intolerance of uncertainty' that has emerged during this same period (Tauritz, 2012). The central argument is that the fluid times in which we live cause many of us to worry about the uncertainty of the future and experience great anxiety (MacLeod, Williams & Bekerian, 1991). This intolerance of uncertainty can be described as "the excessive tendency of an individual to consider it unacceptable that a negative event may occur, however small the probability of its occurrence" (Dugas, Gosselin & Ladouceur, 2001, p. 552). It is not difficult to see how people with a low tolerance of uncertainty may find many aspects of their day-to-day lives quite threatening (Dugas et al., 2001), simply because they cannot be completely known or predicted. In order to reduce this anxiety in children, there are two ways ahead. One is to cocoon them from the uncertainties of the real world; the other is to help them improve the way they negotiate this complex ground.

Tauritz (2012) explains how people today are faced with 'knowledge uncertainty', and argues that they must be taught specific 'uncertainty competences' in order to more effectively think critically about the world around them and then make sound decisions regarding their actions. Situations that are overly predictable will bore students, while those that are too complex and intimidating will elicit feelings of overload (Tauritz, 2012). The key for educators is to root programme design in circumstances that have uncertainty and challenge, so that they arouse curiosity through an appropriate level of cognitive dissonance (Festinger, 1957; Tauritz, 2012; see also Walsh & Golins, 1976).

Tauritz (2012) identified nine uncertainty competences that can be fostered in young people, which can help them reduce, and better tolerate, the uncertainties they face. Of these, some of the most important include being able to accept not knowing what may happen; finding and evaluating information, while judging the sources of this information; assessing one's ability to achieve a particular desired outcome; engaging with a supportive network, and making a plan of action to deal with uncertainty (Tauritz, 2012). These uncertainty competences align with Robinson's (2011) concerns about helping young people develop creative ways of thriving in a rapidly changing and increasingly uncertain world. Our attention now turns to a brief discussion on creativity as a means to enrich adventurous learning.

81

HOW MIGHT WE APPLY THESE PRINCIPLES?

We have suggested that educators need to incorporate uncertainty into their methods of delivery in order to enable our students to better succeed in a world characterized by uncertainty. As with Authenticity and Agency, our pedagogical approach for teaching with uncertainty is not an 'either–or': it lies on a spectrum.

Uncertainty teaching methods are hallmarked by three principal features:

- First, there are multiple courses of action available for students to pursue. There is not one 'right' answer.
- Second, the problem or issue being addressed should be complex enough to demand deep reasoning, but not so full of possibility and choice that it is overwhelming. There must be time and space for 'intelligent deliberation'.
- Third, the educator may not fully know where the educational 'end point' is, nor the path by which it will be reached. The process is uncertain for the educator as well.

At the other end of the Uncertainty spectrum, the features of which we believe should be minimized are lessons that only have room for pre-defined outcomes, tasks that are universalized and 'off the shelf', problems that have only one solution, and situations that demand limited questioning probing, and general 'holistic' engagement (e.g., head, heart and hands).

DISCUSSION

An educational episode that involves considering different courses of action through evaluating sources of evidence and envisioning a variety of different outcomes, has much resonance with the themes we've covered so far. It is authentic, since in the real world, most of our problems (both professional and personal) can be addressed by multiple solutions or a combination of them; students have the power to assess various contrasting and complementary pathways for taking action; and the entire process can be quite challenging, as there may be no precedent of this kind of problem having existed before.

We acknowledge that incorporating elements of uncertainty into a Grade 3 classroom or into an afternoon canoeing session on a lake may not be as straightforward as it sounds. Some outcomes are, and should most definitely be, fixed ahead of time. Educators need to have intended learning intentions and a plan of how they can be effectively reached. However, when this plan obscures students' opportunities to think, experiment and think some more—or blocks students' opportunities to explore other unplanned avenues of learning within the same educational environment—then cause for concern is warranted.

Rather conveniently, it is authentic problems in the real world (discussed in Chapter 5) that often possess the most inherent uncertainty—particularly when compared to the very 'certain' tasks of learning historical facts to be regurgitated on a test paper or rappelling down a rock face. In these cases, one either memorizes enough inert facts to pass the test or not, or decides to feed the rope into the figure 8 device and descend the rope or not. Meaningful learning often does not follow a straight line, yet schooling tries to. Learning in the real world is sometimes frustrating and usually takes a very winding path. The rewards are great, though—especially if it means that students are better equipped to more ably tackle society's most pressing problems, such as climate change, economic inequality and sectarian violence. Indeed, it may be that uncertainty, as a feature of education, requires an element of student responsibility that more conventional approaches do not (Adams, 1995).

Let's now turn to your own practice. If uncertainty is placed on a dimension, where would you place a typical lesson or activity that you teach? How much room was there for students to imagine possible solutions and then develop and refine viable courses of action? Even if there is only one right answer, to what degree was the process of arriving at it open and free? Consider two different ways that you could realistically increase the degree of uncertainty of process or outcome to your lesson plan.

SUMMARY

You should now have an appreciation that uncertainty of process is an integral component of adventurous learning. In this chapter we have discussed how facilitating learning environments requiring students to carefully reason and consider possible courses of action has been discussed by educational philosophers for over two millennia. We saw how dealing with uncertain and 'indeterminate situations' requires imagination, creativity and innovation. Three classic inter-related concepts from foundational psychology (cognitive dissonance, assimilation and accommodation) were then introduced and the roles they play in engaging learners explained. We then discussed the emerging literature that focuses on fostering young people's abilities to tolerate the uncertainties they face (and possibly thrive on them). Finally, some suggestions were presented which can help teachers more deliberately teach with uncertainty as an ally, rather than an undesirable and inescapable feature of life in the 21st century. We now turn to the final element of adventurous learning, which explains the need for learners to be exposed to challenges that require mastery through sustained practice in order to acquire specific knowledge and skills.

Chapter 8

Mastery through Challenge

Every day we face myriad challenges as we go about our daily activities: *How am I going to complete my assignment on time? Will I be able to fit in a workout in my lunch break? How will I manage to complete this pile of marking in the next three days?*

Perhaps you have purposefully set yourself challenges that have taken you beyond your 'comfort zone', such as running a marathon, getting your scuba diving qualification, or learning to play a musical instrument. The challenges that we face may be voluntarily chosen (as in the latter examples), considered part and parcel of modern life (juggling study, part-time work and sports commitments), or they might arrive 'out of the blue' (a career-ending sporting injury, debilitating illness or accident).

The scale of a challenge and how we might deal with it is highly personalized. What might seem to be an insurmountable obstacle or 'the end of the world' for me, might be something that you relish and can't wait to tackle. How we approach a challenge has a lot to do with our attitude, our life experiences and how we might have observed others coping with difficulties. What appears as a challenge might, over time and with sustained practice, become less challenging as our skill set develops.

As discussed earlier, one of the key aspects of good adventure education programmes is that they capture students' attention and involve them in meaningful activities that encourage holistic engagement with the task.

In this chapter we will:

- Discuss the value of appropriate challenges.
- Clearly distinguish between a challenge and concepts of risk and anxiety.

- Explain the importance of mastery.
- Discuss the role of flow as a means to encourage intrinsic motivation.

CHALLENGE

We view challenge as a "demanding task . . . seen as a test of one's abilities" (*OED* online, n.d.). To test or extend one's ability is to build on a foundation of existing knowledge and experience, and to develop new skills which will lead to mastery and a skilful performance. Integral to our conceptualization of challenge in an educational context is the development of skills leading to mastery. This requires the appropriate acquisition of foundational knowledge and skills, the application of time, perseverance in dealing with setbacks, and the support and encouragement of others. Tackling a challenge requires investment on the part of the learner and success is not guaranteed. Luck or external intervention should not be the prime determinants of the outcome.

We do not use challenge interchangeably with risk. While there may be an element of uncertainty regarding what is learned, this is not the driving force, nor the underpinning principle of our conceptualization of challenge. A challenge is within the grasp of abilities of the learner and requires the application of skills and knowledge to achieve the desired outcome. To embark on a challenge does not require the learner to "accept unpleasant feelings of fear, uncertainty and discomfort, and the need for luck", which characterizes Mortlock's (1984) definition of adventure (p. 19). A challenge does not require the learner to possibly suffer physical, mental, social or financial harm in order to learn, nor is a challenge contingent upon the "presence of dangers", which some have claimed is inherent in a risky undertaking (see Priest, 1999, p. 113).

We do not dispute that risks are an inherent aspect of everyday life (just as they are in adventurous learning), however, we believe that the emphasis on risk as a learning strategy is too narrow and restrictive, and frankly, is out-dated. Challenges may involve an element of uncertainty of outcome but they do not require the presence of dangers. For example, a multi-day journey may prove to be challenging for participants without requiring them to be placed in dangerous situations. How one responds to the challenges present in such a journey, both physically and emotionally, may provide many opportunities for learning. Indeed, the absence of physical risks may provide more 'space' for student decision-making and less need for 'expert' intervention. If we are seeking to enable participants to explore cause–effect relationships and to deal with the consequences of their actions, then programmes featuring high levels of perceived risk coupled with low levels of actual risk may be counter-productive, as the focus on 'risky activities' requires high levels of supervision and offers fewer opportunities for students to exercise autonomy.

One approach to providing students with choice regarding the level of challenge is Project Adventure's advocacy of the 'Challenge-by-Choice' principle (Schoel, Prouty & Radcliffe, 1988). This is an attempt to provide students with the opportunity to set their own level of personal challenge —rather than have it imposed on them by someone in authority. While this is well intentioned, the activities over which a learner has choice are still largely determined by outside agents (school teacher or outdoor centre staff), thus the issue of what is an authentic challenge is not addressed. In addition, the choice that is offered is within a novel setting (e.g., challenge course or climbing tower) and the issue of continuity of experi-ence is overlooked.

As Carlson and Evans (2001) rightly point out, Challenge-by-Choice philosophy is based on the idea that participants can make informed choices. However, "A person with little-to-no challenge course experience, or knowledge about course construction, cannot make an informed choice regarding their participation without some information" (Carlson & Evans, 2001, p. 59). We concur with Wolfe and Samdahl's (2005) concern that Challenge-by-Choice assumes that an individual can make a choice. As they point out, "It takes a strong individual to be satisfied with public behavior that one's peers might define as failure" (p. 38).

Peer group pressure can be asserted in both overt and subtle ways and any of us would be naïve to believe that students who are placed in social situations, with peers and other people in positions of authority, will be able to make freely informed decisions that reflect their choice. Seen this way, the notion of Challenge-by-Choice is noble, but, in reality, an individual's capacity to respond to a challenge often made 'on the spot' (e.g., we're now moving to the 'Pamper Pole' element) is both constrained and enabled by social factors, such as the broader cultural norms and personalities within the group. Further, novices do not possess the knowledge and judgment required to undertake their own assessment of the risks associated with the activity and are thus largely "incapable of making a truly informed decision" (Hunt, 1990b, p. 48)

We maintain that issues of choice and challenge lie at a more fundamental level than choosing how to participate on a particular activity; they rest in the choice of the challenge and its relevance to the individual. A meaningful challenge should provide opportunities for learners to first draw on existing skills and knowledge, and then build on these as the task becomes more demanding and complex. Building on existing skills and strengths produces a positive emotional response in learners, which leads to an openness to learn (Passarelli, Hall & Anderson, 2010). Passarelli and colleagues contend that positive emotions broaden a person's perspective and benefits of "fleeting experiences of positive emotions are then stored (i.e., built) to create a reservoir of physical, intellectual and social resources from which individuals draw in future circumstances" (p. 122).

Ideally, the aim of a challenge should be to develop mastery that will allow the learner to use their agency to make informed decisions when faced with choice in authentic learning contexts. Challenges need to be appropriate and educators should be involving learners in negotiating what an 'appropriate challenge' might be. It is important for students to be actively engaged in co-constructing the learning task, rather than being given it by the 'expert'. This approach is supported by Berman and Davis-Berman (2005), who contend that, "when participants are placed in situations with little perceived control and high perceived risk, they may change some behaviors in order to cope and better conform, but these changes will probably not be internalized very well" (p. 20). By being involved in negotiating the challenging task, learners are more likely to have opportunities "to make authentic decisions, to exercise individual and collective agency, and to take some responsibility for their actions" (Brown & Fraser, 2009, p. 73). An educator has an important role in assisting learners to determine an appropriate level of challenge. Too often, groups will be swayed by powerful personalities who are overly ambitious, which then sets the group up for failure. A skilled educator will recognize this and act. Similarly, groups might set their sights too low and be disappointed with failing to really extend themselves. Being open and honest with learners helps them take responsibility and learn more from their decisions.

One of the key differences between a challenging learning experience and a risky one relates to the level of learner autonomy that the former affords. In a challenging environment there should be appropriate progression between the learner's current abilities/skills and their learning trajectory, for which they can take ownership. There is room for experimentation and mistakes; the learners are asked to take responsibility for initiating action and then deal with the consequences. Remember, a challenge should be a demanding task—but this is different from a risky task, where there is the possibility of being harmed. In tasks involving risk, learners have limited opportunities to experiment, as these activities are often in highly orchestrated settings that are far removed from the learner's daily lives. In these situations, learners know that specialist staff will intervene to prevent harm. As a consequence, these risky tasks may be seen as novel thrills which are largely divorced from learners' 'real-life' experiences. Here's an example of what we are talking about.

Imagine a group of 12 students who have been identified as potential school leaders and have been selected to go on a camp. One option would be for them to go to a centre where they would participate in a series of activities that required them to cooperate, communicate and trust one another. It is likely that their programme would be facilitated by a qualified instructor (certainly in any technical activities) and they would be accompanied by a teacher. The students may also be given leadership opportunities (e.g., getting the group organized or leading an initiative activity). This is pretty standard fare and on face value looks to be achieving its goals. After all, the students are communicating, they take their roles as belayers or spotters seriously, and they have a fun time.

But let's dig a little deeper . . . How much choice did the students get to set the agenda? Perhaps they got to state their 'hopes and fears' or have some choice between activities A, B or C. Perhaps they had the responsibility to set the tables before the meal and do the washing up . . . These are examples of students being made to fit into structures and roles that are determined by others. Where, within the script of this style of adventure camp experience, did the students get the opportunity to have a stake in designing a programme that meets their understanding of leadership, trusting other people, or being able to take responsibility of their actions (beyond domestic duties)? What sort of challenges are they facing as potential school leaders? What skills do they already have and how can they be encouraged to develop these through appropriate challenging experiences? This is where a skilful educator is required to listen and work alongside learners, and co-design appropriate challenges. The type of choice that we offer students is important and, as discussed in Chapter 6, meaningful choice is important in fostering agency.

ANXIETY

In many routine activities we may feel a heightened state of anxiety: *Will I make the bus on time? Will my invitation to the movies be accepted? Will I win the online auction for the laptop that I want?* We deal with these day-to-day issues with varying levels of acceptance, resignation or frustration. These are not typically situations in which we purposefully look for feelings of anxiety; these tend to be an undesirable or unwanted by-product. When it comes to advocating the use of challenges in adventurous learning we are very mindful of the balance between positive feelings that come from meeting a challenge and the potential for students to feel threatened and experience unnecessary levels of anxiety.

Elsewhere, Mike has critiqued the notion of pushing students outside their comfort zone in order to learn (Brown, 2008). There are four elements to his critique. First, is the erroneous belief that students learn best when placed in stressful situations; second, is the assumption that outdoor educators are trained and capable of accessing individual students' needs; third, the desire to push students outside their comfort zone has led to the use of increasingly technical activities, which require specialist expertise and thus remove opportunities for students to exercise autonomy; the final part of the comfort zone critique is how the use of activities with a thrill or fear factor (to induce a feeling of being outside one's comfort zone) tends to be 'imposed' on learners, rather than being driven by their needs and aspirations.

A challenge, on the other hand, should start with the learner, build on their strengths and extend their skills and attributes. The learner may wish to explore areas that initially feel uncomfortable, but they are making the choice of how far to extend themself, rather than someone making this decision for them.

A crucial point in this chapter is that challenging activities do not begin with the premise that the learner will be outside their comfort zone as the starting point; this is one significant difference between conventional adventure education and our perspective on adventurous learning. Rather than using stress or dissonance as our starting point, we advocate starting from the learner's strengths and interests and encouraging them to find a challenge that will extend them. The learner might feel some anxiety but it arises from the process of adventurous inquiry. Instead of assuming that stress and anxiety are positive precursors to learning (for critiques see Brown, 2008; Berman & Davis-Berman, 2005; Wolfe & Samdahl, 2005), we are conscious of the fine line that educators and learners both need to tread in order to ensure that learning is an empowering and positive experience, rather than the converse.

Remaining above the 'fine line' has been discussed by British educator Guy Claxton (1984), who suggests that anxiety lies at the boundary between challenge and threat. He notes that "the decision as to whether any learning opportunity constitutes a challenge to be taken up or a threat to be eliminated is a subjective one" (p. 70). He goes on to state that,

> A challenge is a conflict that I hope I can resolve, and feel some confidence in my ability to do so. A threat is a conflict or problem that I do not anticipate being able to sort out through my own efforts, and whose solution is important to my survival. Thus while some problems are threats for almost everyone . . . the variation between people, and between an individual's perceptions at different times, are immense.
>
> (p. 70)

Threats can include harm to a person's physical being as well as one's identity—that is, who a person believes they are. While physical threats are fairly obvious, those relating to one's identity are not as easy to spot, but have equal importance.

Claxton (1984) explains how threats can be negative and damaging. He suggests that,

> *Any* learning situation that threatens to make me incompetent, inconsistent, out of control, and uncomfortable appears to be a threat to me—to my survival as a person I think I am or hope I am or ought to be. When one of these triggers is pulled, learning is resisted, regardless of what the learning is actually about.
>
> (p. 146)

Seen this way, educators have a duty to be sensitive to the difference between what is viewed as a challenge or a threat. Learners involved in a challenge can be encouraged and pushed to extend themselves, while educators need to be conscious of pushing learners too far, too quickly. Claxton (1984) refers to this as 'switching off'.

> 'Switching off' means defending, for example, by going unconscious; and defending is not learning . . . Though from the outside it appears unjustified, defending is *always* appropriate, being the natural response to a perceived threat. If teachers do not spot the shift, and they keep on pushing when a learner is threatened, the learner can very quickly be turned off.
>
> (p. 214)

In our enthusiasm to see participants achieve, we have in the past been guilty of being overly persuasive and pushing students to meet our measure of success, without due regard for the individual's feelings of being threatened. Getting a complete group swiftly through a rappelling session might be rewarding for the instructor, but it isn't necessarily in the best interests of fostering learning for all individuals in the group.

In the desire to see all members of a group 'succeed' it is easy to overlook the potential negative effects of subtle forms of collective pressure from both staff and peers on learners. Zink and Leberman (2001) have highlighted how, "the manipulation of risk can be dysfunctional when the risk is to [sic] great, as this can cause high levels of stress, which in turn may impact negatively on individuals and groups" (p. 52). We consider it important that educators fully consider the potential downsides of placing learners in environments where heightened levels of anxiety and potential for failure might reinforce existing beliefs and compound pre-existing negative feelings of self-worth. As educators we need to be conscious of our expertise, or more specifically our lack of specific training in assessing and managing emotional risk (see Davis-Berman & Berman, 2002). Davis-Berman and Berman have also suggested that, "by intentionally heightening the perception of risk in outdoor programmes, staff may be pushing participants beyond their ability to cope effectively and may be creating unacceptably high levels of anxiety in participants" (p. 30).

Rather than relying on a deficit model, which looks to promote change through a state of "dynamic tension . . . brought about by internal conflict" (Berman & Davis-Berman, 2005, p. 19), adventurous learning looks to build on learners' strengths. Berman and Davis-Berman (2005) have pointed out several problematic aspects of deficit models of change. One important aspect is that "exposure to perceived risk and anxiety can become debilitating for people, working against the process of change. When participants are in such a state of high anxiety that they feel they are in survival mode, meaningful work on issues or change is unlikely" (p. 20).

To be clear, there is a strengthening and more widely held view that the practice of manipulating levels of stress through disequilibrium is questionable and is not a valid rationale for using risk as an aid to learning (Berman & Davis-Berman, 2005; Brown, 2008; Wolfe & Samdahl, 2005). In contrast to much traditional adventure education practice, which places an emphasis on creating a sense of dissonance through the manipulation of risk and anxiety, we believe that more beneficial outcomes will be achieved when learners feel safe, secure and able to take control of their learning, without the risk of suffering physical or emotional harm. Berman and Davis-Berman note that "the greatest amount of change and growth comes from a place of comfort, security and acceptance", so it follows that outdoor educators should "take steps to try to reduce the perception of risk in programs" (p. 22).

A safe and supportive environment provides a sound foundation to develop student agency and autonomy (Martin, 2004). Martin emphasizes that this platform allows teachers to encourage learners to take appropriate risks and be actively involved in self-directed experimentation. In such an approach, students are encouraged to pursue tasks that challenge their existing understandings and help them to realize that learning is sometimes difficult. With support and encouragement, learners are encouraged to experiment and be creative in finding solutions that will enrich their curricular contexts (Martin, 2004).

Skilful educators can assist learners with being increasingly comfortable as they try new solutions and ready themselves to possibly deal with failure. It is through carefully selected challenges that learners can undertake more complex tasks, and in doing so understand that success is not always guaranteed. Dealing with setbacks is part of learning new skills, and being equipped to deal with roadblocks or obstacles is an essential attribute in life. Developing mastery certainly requires the ability to enjoy moments of success and persevere in the face of difficult challenges.

MASTERY

Mastery has been defined as a "consummate skill, ability, or accomplishment" and the "command or comprehensive knowledge *of* a subject, art, or process" (*OED* online, n.d.). If you sit in a handcrafted wooden chair, have a leather satchel or a well-strung tennis racquet, you may well appreciate the level of skill that has been employed to arrive at the final product; you can feel the balance or gaze on the stitching and see the attention to detail. Likewise, you may be a kite surfer, photographer or kayaker who is in control of your equipment, is in tune with the surroundings, and can direct your efforts to achieve your desired goals. Alternatively, you may be able to name every Olympic 100-metre dash champion, the last 20 top-selling songs, or identify the latest model of Ducati motorcycle and recite its key technical data. These are all examples of skills or knowledge that suggest mastery of a topic or activity.

Mastery does not mean that there is nothing more to learn—far from it. But, it does indicate a level of commitment and application over a sustained period. Many of us admire athletes, musicians or artists whose skills and knowledge are not 'natural'; they have been honed to the point of mastery through application and dedication. Mastery comes when people have a passion for a topic or activity and are intrinsically motivated by it. In educational settings, Bohlin et al. (2012) contend that students are more likely to complete tasks and gain mastery if the task is meaningful and presents a challenge. They explain how "emphasizing mastery encourages students to be success-oriented rather than failure-avoiding" (p. 308).

Experiences of mastering a challenge have been shown to lead to improvements in a person's sense of self-efficacy and a reduction in defensive behaviour (Bandura, 1977). We believe there is a sound justification and rationale for the development of skills in adventurous learning. For example, Palmberg and Kuru (2000) found that participation in outdoor activities enhanced learners' relationships with the natural environment. Mullins (2014a) detailed research across a number of activities (e.g., mountaineering, scuba diving, fly fishing, white water kayaking) and showed how skill development enhanced participants' appreciation of, and care for, natural environments. Skills acquired through well-planned adventurous learning programmes can enable learners to be active agents in shaping the world around them (Mullins, 2014b). In the following section we discuss flow theory's contribution to understanding motivation as a key factor in the quest for mastery.

FLOW THEORY

We mentioned Flow theory earlier, but here we get into it in more depth. Flow theory seeks to understand the phenomenon of intrinsic motivation. For example, *Why do rock climbers or painters seemingly lose themselves in their task? What is it about an activity that is so engrossing that one loses sense of time?* According to Flow theory, human behaviour and action are motivated by a desire to achieve a state of flow (Csikszentmihalyi, 1990). When a person is in a state of flow, they are operating at optimum capacity and may 'lose themselves' in the activity. Time seems to stand still, there is an effortlessness to our actions and we may feel at one with our environment. Csikszentmihalyi used the term 'autotelic' to refer to activities that were rewarding in and of themselves, and which elicited the desire to continue. Flow theory helps us build on our earlier discussions concerning the need to facilitate appropriate opportunities to exercise autonomy (see Chapter 6). Achieving flow relies on people perceiving that there are,

> enough opportunities for action (or challenges), which are matched with the person's own capacities to act (or skills). When both challenges and skills are high, the person is not only enjoying the moment, but is also stretching his or her capabilities with the likelihood of learning new skills and increasing self-esteem and personal complexity.
>
> (Csikszentmihalyi & LeFevre, 1989, p. 816)

Central to achieving flow is finding 'an appropriate challenge', where a person's skills can be used and extended. The important point here is the opportunity and the capacity to act based on the learner's needs and desires.

Nakamura and Csikszentmihalyi (2002) have identified the following conditions that are conducive to experiencing flow:

- Perceived challenges, or opportunities for action, that stretch (neither over-matching nor under-utilizing) existing skills; a sense that one is engaging challenges at a level appropriate to one's capacities
- Clear proximal goals and immediate feedback about the progress that is being made.

(p. 90)

Csikszentmihalyi and LeFevre (1989) summarized research confirming that learners felt the most positive conditions for flow existed when both perceived challenges and skills are high and in balance. In this situation, people reported feeling more active, alert, concentrated, happy, satisfied and creative. A central consideration for both people seeking flow, and for educators interested in facilitating it for learners, is finding the balance between tasks that might not contain enough challenge and which result in boredom, and tasks that are too challenging and which lead to damaging levels of anxiety. Neither state produces positive learning outcomes.

We believe that the provision of traditional adventure experiences potentially hinders learners' experiences of flow for the following reasons: the type of activity used has been selected by the instructor; activities have been 'one off' and of short duration, thus students have not had sufficient opportunity to develop skills through autonomous action; the selection of dramatic or novel activities largely precludes students from being able to build on existing skills and knowledge—an adrenaline rush or 'buzz', while highly emotive, is not the same as flow. Adventure activity providers are very proficient at creating fun thrilling activities, but the very nature of short-duration sessions (e.g., a 3-hour rock climbing session, which may only involve 20 minutes of climbing activity per student), by definition severely limits the development of skills and judgment that have been identified as leading to the flow state. It is our view that facilitating learners' experiences of flow, through challenges and the achievement of mastery, is a crucial role of the educator in adventurous learning.

It is worth quoting a long passage from Nakamura and Csikszentmihalyi (2002), where they clearly state the learning possibilities made available through achieving flow:

> The flow state is intrinsically rewarding and leads the individual to seek to replicate flow experiences; this introduces a selective mechanism into psychological functioning that fosters growth. As people master challenges in an activity, they develop greater levels of skill, and the activity ceases to be as involving as before. In order to continue experiencing flow, they must identify and engage progressively more complex challenges . . . A flow activity not only provides a set of challenges or opportunities for action but it typically also provides a system of graded challenges, able to accommodate a person's continued and deepening enjoyment as skills grow.
>
> (p. 92)

Nakamura and Csikszentmihalyi (2002) go on to describe what is effectively a 'virtuous circle', where challenge and mastery lead to the seeking of further challenges and the development of more complex skills. Berman and Davis-Berman (2005) have suggested that outdoor educators would better served by focusing on the provision of autotelic experiences (which are intrinsically rewarding and which people want more of), rather than trying to bring about change by manipulating various elements of a 'learning experience', such as perceived risk. They suggest that autotelic experiences can be facilitated by helping learners enjoy suitably challenging activities and developing useful skills in a supportive environment.

Flow theory supports the pedagogy of adventurous learning and the call for appropriate challenges that build on and extend learners' current abilities and skills. Central to this foundation is the importance of learner-derived challenges, as opposed to those imposed by (well-meaning) educators.

DISCUSSION

Throughout this chapter we have built a case for using appropriate learner-centred challenges that build on, and extend, skills leading to mastery. Rather than specifying a list of educator-determined tasks, we argue for the importance of negotiated or co-constructed challenges. As Fraser (2008) reminds us,

> We do our students no favours when we mistake entertainment for education and when we convey that learning should be fun. Entertainment is a short-lived pleasure whereas education requires sustained effort (Katz, 2002). Sometimes we forget about the struggle that is part of the satisfaction of learning . . . Striking the optimum conditions for challenge is part of the art of teaching.
>
> (p. 9)

In adventurous learning we should provide learners with favourable conditions for authentic and meaningful experiences where they are challenged in an appropriate manner with suitable support (Brown, 2008). Creating an environment where learners feel able to move beyond what they know, to question and to speculate without fear or risk of being wrong, needs to be a primary aim for all educators (Costa & Kallick, 2000; Brown & Fraser, 2009). Educational theory attests to the value of challenges (Costa & Kallick, 2000; Sternberg, 2000) with the intention of building resilience in the face of setbacks and frustration (Claxton, 2002). Resilience requires the learner to persevere at things that are challenging and to tolerate the feelings that inevitably accompany difficulties (Brown & Fraser, 2009).

As previously discussed, learners are more likely to be intrinsically motivated to perform activities when they feel they have autonomy. Autonomy is based on the ability to make informed decisions based on one's competence and probability of success (Bohlin et al., 2012). Competence is based on the development of suitable skills (leading to mastery) from which informed judgments can be made. Central to this educational scaffolding is the development of incremental challenges whereby learners feel competent, have a reasonable expectation of being able to meet the challenges they face, and have opportunities to experience enough flow, which will in turn stimulate intrinsic motivation to continue to learn.

We now invite you to reflect on your own practice and ask you to think of the ways in which your teaching features challenges that demand mastery of skills and knowledge. Where do your lessons and activity sessions lie on the Mastery dimension? To what degree is prolonged, deep engagement with the content required to face what is hopefully a series of progressive challenges? Think of two specific ways that you could revise your delivery of a curricular area so that it demands mastery and decision-making based on the knowledge and skills acquired.

SUMMARY

In this chapter we discussed the educational imperatives of students encountering and dealing with appropriate challenges. Educators are again faced with making important judgments about what might be considered by learners to be challenging rather than threatening. We also introduced literature outlining the importance of mastery. It is this mastery of skills and knowledge that enables learners to overcome challenges. Too often, conventional adventure activity programmes involving height, moving water or steep ground are so controlled by 'expert instructors', that most participants could not possibly have the required skills and knowledge to take part in the activity without large amounts of technical supervision. Finally, we discussed the role of flow as a means to foster intrinsic motivation. Flow involves receiving immediate feedback on performance and can lead to feelings of accomplishment, which in turn leads to learners wanting to engage further.

We now turn to the final chapter, where we explain how the four dimensions of adventurous learning can be considered as a coherent pedagogical approach.

Chapter 9

Adventurous Learning

Weaving the Strands Together

Education is far from a simple enterprise, despite the occasional rallying call from politicians to get back to the basics—sometimes referred to as the '3Rs' of Reading, Writing and Arithmetic. While competency in basic numeracy and literacy may be useful in societies with economies based in mass production and manufacture, these skills alone are not sufficient to prepare students for a future marked by increasingly rapid shifts in the cultural, economic and environmental spheres. As we explained in Chapter 3, contemporary society is characterized by fluidity—in family structures, career trajectories, leisure choices and ways in which we construct and maintain our sense of identity. Throughout the preceding chapters we have outlined the challenges and opportunities presented by this shifting landscape and we have detailed the inadequacies of current forms of educational practice. In a world that is underpinned by uncertainty, recourse to simplistic solutions, such as getting back to the 3Rs, are just that—simplistic. For as Henry Mencken, 'the Sage of Baltimore', is reported to have said, "For every complex problem there is an answer that is clear, simple, and wrong."[1]

In this final chapter we will:

- Argue that the four dimensions of adventurous learning come with ethical imperatives.
- Provide a synthesis of how the four dimensions can be used to consider the degree to which our current and future programmes can be considered adventurous.

- Summarize the book's key arguments and make closing comments.

ADVENTUROUS LEARNING AS AN ETHICAL ENTERPRISE

As educators, we have been concerned that neo-liberal policies and the increasing commodification of education exist to the detriment of the young people who are seeking purpose in their schooling experiences. In both in-class and outdoor settings we have observed learning experiences becoming increasingly constrained by institutional imperatives (e.g., strict operating procedures and standardized assessment tasks) that together create a disjuncture between education and learners' everyday lives.

As we argued in Chapter 4, many forms of adventure education—that on first glance could be the alternative vision to the malaise of mainstream education—have been 'hollowed out' and stripped of meaningful opportunities for students to be agents of their learning in authentic settings. The commodification of 'adventure experiences' restricts opportunities for learners to develop mastery, and therefore truncates the potential for ongoing, self-directed learning.

In our vision of adventurous learning we have defined four key components: authenticity, agency, uncertainty and mastery—which together underpin our conception of adventure in an educational context. We don't pretend that a modest textbook will change the dominant educational discourses that overtly and subtly shape social structures, policy and individual behaviours. What we are encouraging, however, is a conscious reconsideration of the role of adventure in educational contexts and how we might facilitate experiences that open up possibilities for different ways of learning about and knowing the world. This reconsideration is positioned as a counter-movement to the ethically suspect educational systems that restrict student learning on the basis of what is easiest to control and what costs the least amount of money. Adventures, we argue, need to be repositioned as fertile grounds for people to discover the world they inhabit and their capacity they possess to live well in it.

The notion of 'living well' is central to our educational endeavour. Inherent in this notion is the ethical imperative that is interwoven through Chapters 5–8, where we outline the four dimensions of adventurous learning.

This chapter presents the four dimensions of adventurous learning in a diagram. We have provided this diagram to help educators critically reflect on, and possibly reframe, their pedagogical approach. In presenting this diagram we had extensive discussions around how it might be interpreted, or more importantly, how it might be misinterpreted. As professionals in the field of education we are constantly required to make decisions that influence the human and non-human communities which we inhabit. This diagram is not to be 'imposed on' learners, for to do so would be to replicate the problematic practices that have led adventure education into its current *cul de sac*.

Our intention is for this diagram to be used as a reflective tool, in which the needs and aspirations of your learners remain at the forefront of the decisions you make concerning what adventurous learning might 'look like' in your contexts. In this light, adopting an adventurous learning approach involves a careful negotiation between what is possible and what is desirable—between being pragmatic and determining what is a 'bottom line'. Consideration of the need to 'live well' rests in addressing social inequalities and access to adventurous learning, connecting learning to community needs and aspirations, and ensuring that learning experiences foster an ethic of care to both the human and non-human worlds. In other words, adventurous learning is, by its very being, a form of place-responsive education: it is responsive to the *Where?*, the *Who?*, and the *To what end?* issues of education.

ILLUSTRATING THE FOUR DIMENSIONS OF ADVENTUROUS LEARNING

It is our contention that adventurous learning should not be restricted to a set of prescribed activities, nor is it a simple 'cut and paste' model that is applied without due consideration to context. In valuing the professionalism of educators, we encourage readers to carefully consider the needs of their students, the physical setting, their skills and the resources that are available. The four concepts of authenticity, agency, uncertainty and mastery through challenge are not prescriptive, and the degree to which any are present will depend on the learning intentions for a particular lesson or series of lessons. The key, we believe, is to consider how combinations of these four concepts can be more deliberately incorporated into challenging learning experiences.

Let's begin this section by looking at Figure 9.1.

Figure 9.1 shows four dimensions, with higher levels of each element being closer to the centre. Although we normally approach models such as this with a measure of caution (usually because they over-simplify

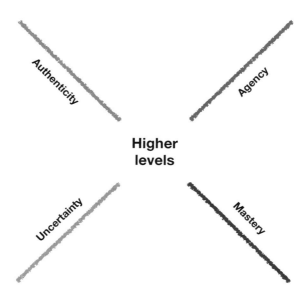

Figure 9.1 Adventurous learning considered on four dimensions

complex ideas), we want the concepts presented in this book to be applicable to your educational practice, and so it felt right to illustrate them—particularly as visualization is an important aid to learning for many people.

We'll now present four different examples that will show how the model can be put into practice. We've chosen two examples that demonstrate low levels of adventurous learning, and two that are more closely aligned with our philosophy.

The first scenario is at a small lake at an outdoor centre, where a class of 15-year-olds is divided in four groups of six. Their instructor has set a task that requires each group to build a raft with the rope, barrels and bamboo poles that were provided. They are then to paddle the raft to an island that is 200 metres away. We've placed a marker on each of the four dimensions in order to reflect one view of the 'adventurousness' of the raft-building exercise (see Figure 9.2).

From our perspective, it is very unlikely that students will need to know how to build a sea-worthy raft in order to thrive in the 21st century. Therefore, this is low on the authenticity dimension. The task was not determined by the participants, so right away their capacity to exercise agency, beyond completing the immediate task, was diminished. The good

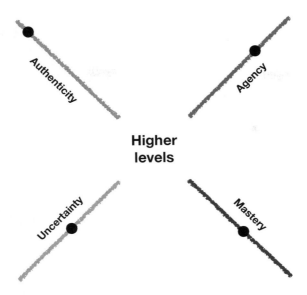

Figure 9.2 Raft-building exercise mapped on dimensions

news is that they can make choices in terms of the way they use the material. The level of uncertainty is the activity's most redeeming feature, as it is not certain that the participants will be able to construct a raft that will allow them to paddle to the island without getting wet. Also in its favour is the way the task demands imagination, creativity and innovation; the teams will need to come up with ideas and then test and refine them, before committing to a final design. Finally, some mastery may be required, in terms of learning some knots and hitches for the raft's construction. Still, the usefulness of this form of mastery may be quite limited beyond the confines of this rather contrived setting. We do acknowledge that there is the potential for students to build on skills associated with improving communication and perhaps developing leadership. But, given the difficulties that have been shown to exist in learners recognizing similarities in different contexts and then being able to transfer these skills, we would be very cautious about over-inflating claims that students gain mastery in these domains.

Do you agree with our analysis of the raft-building exercise? We suspect that you don't agree completely and that you might respond with 'well, it depends'. In truth, we are not particularly worried about exactly where on the dimensions most common adventure-based and classroom-based activities lie. This model can be viewed as a resource that you and your colleagues can use to have discussions about the degree to which your sessions incorporate elements of adventurous learning and how you might deliberately try to increase the level on some of the dimensions. Please keep this in mind for the following three examples, as we have included them to illustrate the process of systematic, critical reflection, rather than as definitive exemplars.

The next example is of a class of 8th Graders who are approximately 14 years old. Their teacher challenged them with devising a self-propelled journey that would start at a point of interest and finish at their suburban school, and which would involve an overnight stay.

The students decided to paddle two 12-person canoes down the nearby, slow-moving river. They arranged for a minibus and trailer to take them to a public park that was 25 miles upstream of a park where they could do some paddling practice and then launch the boats. Their take-out point was 2 miles by path and road to their school. About halfway along their route was an old church that a couple of the children attended with their families. The children negotiated with the minister the use of the adjacent building, which comprised a couple of multi-purpose rooms, a kitchen and eating area. This allowed the boys' group and girls' group to sleep on the floors of separate rooms and for the class to be able to cook and eat under shelter. There was no religious aspect to their stay.

Although the canoe journey was somewhat contrived, it would not be unusual for people to canoe on that stretch of river. Indeed, canoeing is a recreational activity in which some students may already take part and which some may choose to do in their own leisure time in the coming years. Travelling through and exploring the environs of one's community also has a stronger resonance with the daily lives of those who live locally (as the students do); they were getting to know 'their place'. The students had a fair degree of agency in that they chose the mode of travel and they arranged the logistics associated with ground transport, accommodation and food. Adults were needed to supervise the paddling, cooking and the sleeping-over elements, but their role was more of guides than 'commanders'. There was not a huge amount of uncertainty in the outcome, but every step of the way involved some uncertainty of process, as the tasks involved in addressing the overall challenge of travelling from point A to point B were not entirely the same ones students had faced before. Finally, the project involved building upon existing canoeing, cooking and negotiating skills, through direct and real-world application that could continue being developed after the project ended (see Figure 9.3).

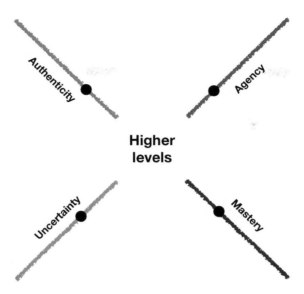

Figure 9.3 Canoe journey mapped on dimensions

The third scenario is of a Grade 6 geometry class, where students are being taught how to calculate the perimeter and area of basic shapes like rectangles and cubes. The teacher has taught them the theory, which they have then used to complete ten questions on a worksheet.

We should start by stating that we are not 'having a dig' at mathematics —although math classes often make for an easy target, when they don't need to be. Numeracy skills are a vital part of a child's education, as they are used frequently, in countless aspects of daily living. Back to the geometry scenario: there is very little that is authentic in being given a worksheet consisting of abstract problems (e.g., ones that have no relevance to the students' lives) as a means of 'reinforcing' learning. The students had almost no agency in any part of this lesson; they could have chosen not to comply, but that might have had negative sanctions attached to it (e.g., an after-school detention). There was almost no possibility of an uncertain outcome or creative processes being marshalled to arrive at the correct answer. This particular geometry class probably rates highest on the mastery dimension, as presumably the content of the class in question built upon what was learned in yesterday's class and will inform what is learned in tomorrow's (see Figure 9.4). So, there is some Deweyan (1938/1997) continuity.

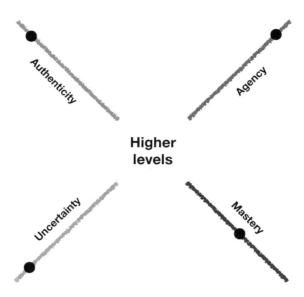

Figure 9.4 Geometry class mapped on dimensions

Still, wouldn't it have been interesting to see how that class's content might have been covered by allowing students to first identify the multitude of squares and rectangles that can be spotted from the school grounds, then choose ten for closer examination, and then go back to the classroom to calculate the perimeter and area of each? This simple tweak of the algebra class can increase its degree of authenticity, agency and uncertainty.

Our fourth and final scenario that will be used to illustrate our conception of adventurous learning is one that focuses on the Outdoor Journeys approach that was developed at the University of Edinburgh (www.outdoor journeys.org.uk). This approach involves students asking historical and ecological questions about the local landscape, doing research to find the answer and then sharing their knowledge with others through different forms of media. In this scenario, a class of Grade 5 students went to explore their school grounds in pairs. Each pair came back to the class with a list of questions they had about the landscape they visited almost every day, and posted their two favourite questions on the classroom wall. One pair's two questions were: *What was on this land before there was a school?* and *What kind of tree is that big one by the main gate?*

The students found the answer to the first question by referring to a copy of an old map of the area that the teacher had placed on the resource table.

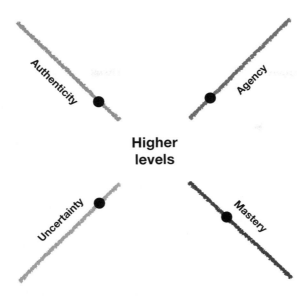

Figure 9.5 Outdoor Journeys session mapped on dimensions

Their second answer came from a tree identification fold-out card that was also on the table. The students decided to share the answer to their first question by taking a photograph of the map and projecting it on the class screen using Powerpoint. They decided for a low-tech approach for sharing the second answer, and simply explained to the class how they had deduced the type of tree with the fold-out card by following a few easy steps.

As you can see, the Outdoor Journeys session rates highly on all four dimensions of adventurous learning (see Figure 9.5). First, this kind of schooling is entirely located in phenomena that are encountered on a daily basis. Levels of agency are high, as the students had plenty of autonomy with which to choose what they wanted to learn about; they could follow their passions and interest. There was a high degree of uncertainty—not least for the teacher, as he had little idea of where the students' curiosity would take them. The teacher's role was one of facilitator, rather than 'content expert' and 'imparter of knowledge'. Finally, a fair degree of mastery was demanded, as the students needed to develop skills to interpret an old map, understand how to use a tree identification tool and project an image of their map on to the screen.

Central to our summary of this chapter's first section on how to let the four dimensions serve you and your practice is that our schematic diagram is a very basic tool. It has been put forward as an instrument that can enable educators to more systematically reflect on why they deliver elements of content in certain ways—and how they might make a conscious effort to make their teaching more adventurous. Along with this individual reflection, we hope that this diagram will lie at the heart of some fiery and productive debate among practitioners. We're completely aware, though, that what lies at the heart of our diagram (e.g., the higher end of the dimensions) may not be feasible for some educators, simply due to constraints put on them by regulations (e.g., state tests) or cultural norms (e.g., 'we've always done things this way and we're not about to change').

The diagram and the theory that underpins adventurous learning should not lead to a recipe book approach; together they represent a way of critiquing and developing methods of providing students with the kinds of learning that will be most useful to them throughout their school life and beyond.

ADVENTUROUS LEARNING: POSSIBILITIES AND POTENTIAL

The majority of this chapter has focused on how the four dimensions can be used to more deeply consider four different educational scenarios. Just as we did in Chapter 3, let's now take a look outwards and consider how adventurous learning programmes may be more firmly located within wider educational and socio-cultural contexts. In this light, two principal starting points are that, (1) adventurous learning is accessible to a broad range of socio-economic and cultural groups, and (2) adventurous learning is strongly aligned with sustainability-focused, low-carbon pursuits that have minimal dependence on fossil fuels for equipment production and transport. Inherent in these principles is Dewey's (1938) call to embed teaching and learning within local communities. Finally, we see adventurous learning being compatible with the digital technologies that imbue so many aspects of our lives—not least because the 'digital natives' with whom we work will find a natural resonance with these methodologies.

In our own work we have 'played with' and developed the principles of adventurous learning over several years (Beames, 2006; Beames & Ross, 2010; Brown, 2012a, 2012b). A large driver of these initiatives has been the desire to democratize outdoor learning so that as wide a group of students as possible can participate in meaningful educational experiences. By localizing learning, drawing on students' and teachers' knowledge and providing opportunities for cross-curricular engagement, we have seen first-hand how adventurous learning can enhance student–teacher relationships. In addition, it strengthens students' connections with their local places by embedding curriculum content that is engaging and meaningful (e.g., water quality analysis showed high levels of pollution and led to increased environmental citizenship). Conventional forms of residential outdoor education provision were beyond the financial reach of many students' families and, given the cultural diversity within the student cohort, many traditional adventure activities were viewed by young people as less appealing, irrelevant and even 'common' (e.g., we rappelled and built the raft last year and the year before that).

Our attempts to reshape what adventurous learning can be have allowed us to develop programmes, in collaboration with the teachers, that encouraged greater student agency (e.g., organizing food, driving curriculum through their curious questioning); higher levels of authenticity (e.g., learning about the math, geography, history and science existing in their 'places', and addressing current local issues); building and exercising mastery (e.g., paddling waka (Māori canoes), recording and interpreting meteorological data from the schools' weather station); and uncertainty of process (e.g., teachers stepping back and leaving space for students to be imaginative and make considered decisions). Programmes were based on the students' everyday contexts and their needs, and did not focus on 'squeezing' them into a series of predetermined activities. One of the big upsides of this approach is the reduction in CO_2 emissions from transport and the less obvious, but nevertheless important, aspect of not needing expensive investment in infrastructure (e.g., dedicated buildings and specialist equipment) that also have ongoing detrimental environmental impacts.

CONCLUDING COMMENTS

Adventurous learning is more than a semantic twist; it is an earnest attempt to engage students and teachers in an approach to education that aims to maximize participation and learning in a world that is constantly changing—a world of ambiguity and uncertainty in which we can be agents of change rather than passive recipients of dominant forms of knowledge and social norms.

Our belief is that adventurous learning offers educators of all kinds guidelines that can influence their teaching: to help keep the learning real, to give children power, to ensure that the outcomes are not predetermined, and to provide opportunities to develop their capacity to master crucial lifelong skills. Robinson (2011) notes that the earth's population is now facing some incredibly daunting challenges. We agree with his belief that in education lies the resources needed to cultivate children's "abilities of imagination, creativity and innovation"; indeed, "the stakes could hardly be higher" (p. 47).

Our role as 'facilitators of rich learning experiences' is to foster opportunities for our students to be immersed in educational settings that encourage moral growth, positive social interaction, and the knowledge and skills to effectively address the situations they encounter. As educators, we are all required to go on our own adventurous learning journey—a journey full of uncertainty, but one with a clear outcome: to do our best to engage with students in the present, so that they develop the attributes and skills needed to flourish as individuals, and participate fully, within a civil and just society. The dimensions of adventurous learning provide a readily applicable framework for you to use in your efforts to reshape the educational landscape.

NOTE

1   http://www.brainyquote.com/quotes/quotes/h/hlmencke129796.html#llgp B7TcOzusfJtJ.99.

References

Adams, J. (1995). *Risk*. London: UCL Press.

Allison, P. & Telford, J. (2005). Turbulent times: Outdoor education in Great Britain, 1993–2003. *Australian Journal of Outdoor Education, 9*, 21–30.

Aoki, T. (1993). Legitimating lived curriculum: Towards a curricular landscape of multiplicity. *Journal of Curriculum and Supervision, 8*(3), 255–268.

Assor, A., Kaplan, H. & Roth, G. (2002). Choice is good, but relevance is excellent: Autonomy-enhancing and suppressing teacher behaviours predicting students' engagement in schoolwork. *British Journal of Educational Psychology, 72*, 261–278.

Bandura, A. (1977). Self-efficacy: Towards a unifying theory of behavioural change. *Psychological Review, 84*(2), 191–215.

Bandura, A. (1982). Self-efficacy mechanism in human agency. *American Psychologist, 37*(2), 122–147.

Barnett, R. (2000). University knowledge in an age of supercomplexity. *Higher Education, 40*, 409–422.

Bauman, Z. (2007). *Liquid Times: Living in an Age of Uncertainty*. Cambridge: Polity Press.

Beames, S. (2006). Losing my religion: The struggle to find applicable theory. *Pathways: The Ontario Journal of Outdoor Education, 19*(1), 4–11.

Beames, S., Atencio, M. & Ross, H. (2009). Taking excellence outdoors. *Scottish Educational Review, 41*(2), 32–45.

Beames, S. & Brown, M. (2014). Enough of Ronald and Mickey: Focusing on learning in outdoor education. *Journal of Adventure Education and Outdoor Learning, 14*(2), 118–131.

Beames, S., Higgins, P. & Nicol, R. (2011). *Learning Outside the Classroom*. New York: Routledge.

Beames, S. & Pike, E.J. (2013). Introduction. In E.J. Pike & S. Beames (eds), *Outdoor Adventure and Social Theory* (pp. 1–9). London: Routledge.

111

Beames, S. & Ross, H. (2010). Journeys outside the classroom. *Journal of Adventure Education and Outdoor Learning, 10*(2), 95–109.

Beck, U. (1992). *Risk Society: Towards a New Modernity*. London: Sage.

Becker, P. (2003). The intense longing for authenticity or why people seek out adventure. In B. Humberstone, H. Brown & K. Richards (eds), *Whose Journeys? The Outdoors and Adventure as Social and Cultural Phenomena* (pp. 91–104). Penrith: Institute for Outdoor Learning.

Becker, P. (2008). The curiosity of Ulysses and its consequences: In search of the educational myth of the adventure. In P. Becker & J. Schirp (eds), *Other Ways of Learning* (pp. 199–209). Marburg: European Institute for Outdoor Adventure Education and Experiential Learning.

Beedie, P. & Bourne, G. (2005). Media constructions of risk: A case study of the Stainforth Beck incident. *Journal of Risk Research, 8*(4), 331–339.

Berman, D. & Davis-Berman, J. (2005). Positive psychology and outdoor education. *Journal of Experiential Education, 28*(1), 17–24.

Black, A. & Deci, E. (2000). The effects of instructors' autonomy support and students' autonomous motivation on learning organic chemistry: A self-determination theory perspective. *Science Education, 84*(6), 740–756.

Blank, M. & Berg, A. (2006). *All Together Now: Sharing Responsibility for the Whole Child*. Washington, DC: Coalition for Community Schools.

Blumer, H. (1969). *Symbolic Interactionism: Perspective and Method*. Berkeley, CA: University of California Press.

Bohlin, L., Durwin, C. & Reese-Weber, M. (2012). *EdPsych Modules* (2nd edn). New York: McGraw-Hill Higher Education.

Bonnett, M. & Cuypers, S. (2002). Autonomy and authenticity in education. In N. Blake, P. Smeyer, R. Smith & P. Standish (eds), *The Blackwell Guide to the Philosophy of Education* (pp. 326–340). Oxford: Blackwell.

van Bottenburg, M. & Salome, L. (2010). The indoorisation of outdoor sports: An exploration of the rise of lifestyle sports in artificial settings. *Leisure Studies, 29*(2), 143–160.

Boud, D., Cohen, R. & Walker, D. (1993). *Using Experience for Learning*. Buckingham: Open University Press.

Brennan, A. (1994). Environmental literacy and the educational ideal. *Environmental Values, 3*(1), 3–16.

Brookes, A. (2003a). A critique of Neo-Hahnian outdoor education theory. Part one: Challenges to the concept of "character building". *Journal of Adventure Education and Outdoor Learning, 3*(1), 49–62.

Brookes, A. (2003b). A critique of Neo-Hahnian outdoor education theory. Part two: "The fundamental attribution error" in contemporary outdoor education discourse. *Journal of Adventure Education and Outdoor Learning, 3*(2), 119–132.

Brown, M. (2008). Comfort zone: Model or metaphor? *Australian Journal of Outdoor Education, 12*(1), 3–12.

Brown, M. (2010). Transfer: Outdoor adventure education's Achilles heel? Changing participation as a viable option. *Australian Journal of Outdoor Education, 14*(1), 13–22.

Brown, M. (2012a). A changing landscape: Place responsive pedagogy. In D. Irwin, J. Straker & A. Hill (eds), *Outdoor Education in Aotearoa New Zealand: A New Vision for the Twenty First Century* (pp. 104–124). Christchurch: Christchurch Polytechnic Institute of Technology.

Brown, M. (2012b). Student perspectives of a place-responsive outdoor education programme. *New Zealand Journal of Outdoor Education, 3*(1), 64–88.

Brown, M. (2013). Teacher perspectives on place-responsive outdoor education. *Set, 3,* 3–10.

Brown, M. & Fraser, D. (2009). Re-evaluating risk and exploring educational alternatives. *Journal of Adventure Education and Outdoor Learning, 9*(1), 61–77.

Bryman, A. (1999). The Disneyization of society. *Sociological Review, 47*(1), 25–47.

Bryman, A. (2004). *The Disneyization of Society.* London: Sage.

Buckley, R. (2012). Rush as a key motivation in skilled adventure tourism: Resolving the risk recreation paradox. *Tourism Management, 33,* 961–970.

Butin, D.W. (2010). *Service-learning in Theory and Practice: The Future of Community Engagement in Higher Education.* New York: Palgrave Macmillan.

Buzzelli, C. & Johnston, B. (2001). Authority, power, and morality in classroom discourse. *Teaching and Teacher Education, 17*(8), 873–884.

Capra, F. (1997). *The Web of Life: A New Synthesis of Life and Matter.* London: Flamingo.

Carlson, J. & Evans, K. (2001). Whose choice is it? Contemplating challenge-by-choice and diverse-abilities. *Journal of Experiential Education, 24*(1), 58–63.

Cater, C. (2006). Playing with risk? Participant perceptions of risk and management implications in adventure tourism. *Tourism Management, 27,* 316–325.

Cater, C. & Dash, G. (2013). Alienation and false consciousness in adventurous activities. In E.J. Pike & S. Beames (eds), *Outdoor Adventure and Social Theory* (pp. 13–22). London: Routledge.

Centre for Occupational Research & Development. (n.d.). *Contextual learning.* Retrieved from http://www.cord.org/contextual-learning-definition/

Claxton, G. (1984). *Live and Learn: An Introduction to the Psychology of Growth and Change in Everyday Life.* London: Harper and Row.

Claxton, G. (2002). *Building Learning Power.* Bristol: The Learning Organisation.

Claxton, G. (2012). Virtues of uncertainty. *Aeon.* Retrieved from http://aeon.co/magazine/society/guy-glaxton-education-morality-character/

Costa, A. & Kallick, B. (eds). (2000). *Activating and Engaging Habits of Mind.* Alexandria, VA: Association for Supervision and Curriculum Development.

Crocco, M. & Costigan, A. (2007). The narrowing of curriculum and pedagogy in the age of accountability: Urban educators speak out. *Urban Education, 42*(6), 512–535.

Csikszentmihalyi, M. (1990). *Flow.* New York: Harper and Row.

Csikszentmihalyi, M. (1996). *Creativity: Flow and the Psychology of Discovery and Invention.* New York: Harper Collins.

Csikszentmihalyi, M. (2000). *Beyond Boredom and Anxiety.* San Francisco, CA: Jossey-Bass.

113

Csikszentmihalyi, M. & LeFevre, J. (1989). Optimal experience in work and leisure. *Journal of Personality and Social Psychology, 56*(5), 815–822.

Davis, B. & Sumara, D. (2006). *Complexity and Education: Inquiries into Learning, Teaching and Research.* Mahwah, NJ: Erlbaum.

Davis-Berman, J. & Berman, D. (2002). Risk and anxiety in adventure programming. *Journal of Experiential Education, 25*(2), 305–310.

Dearden, R.F. (1972). Autonomy and education. In R. Dearden, P. Hirst & R. Peters (eds), *Education and the Development of Reason* (pp. 58–75). London: Routledge & Kegan Paul.

Deci, E. & Ryan, R. (1987). The support of autonomy and the control of behavior. *Journal of Personality and Social Psychology, 53*(6), 1024–1037.

DeFalco, A. (2010). An analysis of John Dewey's notion of occupations: Still pedagogically valuable? *Education & Culture, 26*(1), 82–99.

Detterman, D. (1993). The case for the prosecution: Transfer as an epiphenomenon. In D. Detterman & R. Sternberg (eds), *Transfer on Trial: Intelligence, Cognition, and Instruction* (pp. 1–24). Norwood, NJ: Ablex.

Dettweiler, U., Ünlü, A., Lauterbach, G., Becker, C. & Gschrey, B. (2015). Investigating the motivational behavior of pupils during outdoor science teaching within self-determination theory. *Frontiers in Psychology, 6*(125), 1–16.

Dewey, J. (1897). My pedagogic creed. *School Journal, 54*(3), 77–80.

Dewey, J. (1915/1990). *The School and Society.* Chicago, IL: University of Chicago Press.

Dewey, J. (1916/2004). *Democracy and Education.* Mineola, NY: Dover.

Dewey, J. (1922). *Human Nature and Conduct: An Introduction to Social Psychology.* New York: Henry Holt & Co.

Dewey, J. (1938/1997). *Experience and Education.* New York: Touchstone.

Dewey, J. (1938). *Logic: The Theory of Inquiry.* New York: Henry Holt and Co.

Dickson, T.J. & Gray, T. (2006). Facilitating experiences: A snap shot of what is happening out there. *Australian Journal of Outdoor Education, 10*(2), 41–52.

Dirkx, J.M., Amey, M. & Haston, L. (1999). Context in the contextualized curriculum: Adult life worlds as unitary or multiplistic? In A. Austin, G.E. Nynes & R.T. Miller (eds), *Proceedings of the 18th Annual Midwest Research to Practice Conference in Adult, Continuing, and Community Education* (pp. 79–84). St. Louis: University of Missouri at St. Louis. ERIC Document Reproduction Service No. ED 447 269.

Duckworth, E. (2011). *The Having of Wonderful Ideas* (3rd edn). New York: Teachers College Press.

Dugas, M.J., Gosselin, P. & Ladouceur, R. (2001). Intolerance of uncertainty and worry: Investigating specificity in a nonclinical sample. *Cognitive Therapy and Research, 25*(5), 551–558.

Ede, A. (2006). Scripted curriculum: Is it a prescription for success? *Childhood Education, 83*(1), 29–32.

Edwards, B. & Corte, U. (2010): Commercialization and lifestyle sport: Lessons from 20 years of freestyle BMX in "Pro-Town, USA". *Sport in Society, 13*(7–8), 1135–1151.

Elias, N. & Dunning, E. (1986). *The Quest for Excitement: Sport and Leisure in the Civilising Process.* Oxford: Blackwell.

Elliot, A. (2014). *Contemporary Social Theory* (2nd edn). London: Routledge.

Elliot, A. & Urry, J. (2010). *Mobile Lives.* London: Routledge.

Fägerstam, E. (2014). High school teachers' experience of the educational potential of outdoor teaching and learning. *Journal of Adventure Education and Outdoor Learning, 14*(1), 56–81.

Farley, R. (2005). "By endurance we conquer": Ernest Shackleton and performances of white male hegemony. *International Journal of Cultural Studies, 8*(2), 231–245.

Festinger, L. (1957). *A Theory of Cognitive Dissonance.* Stanford, CA: Stanford University Press.

Fletcher, R. (2010). The Emperor's new adventure: Public secrecy and the paradox of adventure tourism. *Journal of Contemporary Ethnography, 39*(1), 6–33.

Foley, M., Frew, M. & McGillivray, D. (2003). Rough comfort: Consuming adventure on the 'edge'. In B. Humberstone, H. Brown & K. Richards (eds), *Whose Journeys? The Outdoors and Adventure as Social and Cultural Phenomena* (pp. 149–160). Penrith: Institute of Outdoor Learning.

Fraser, D. (2008). Developing classroom culture: Creating a climate for learning. In C. McGee & D. Fraser (eds), *The Professional Practice of Teaching* (pp. 1–16). Melbourne: Cengage.

Freire, P. (1970/1993). *Pedagogy of the Oppressed* (M. Bergman Ramos, trans.). New York: Continuum.

Garrison, J. (1997). *Dewey and Eros: Wisdom and Desire in the Art of Teaching.* New York: Teachers College Press.

Garrison, J. (1999). John Dewey's theory of practical reasoning. *Educational Philosophy and Theory, 31*(3), 291–312.

Gass, M.A. (1985). Programming the transfer of learning in adventure education. *Journal of Experiential Education, 8*(3), 18–24.

Gass, M.A. & Stevens, C. (2007). Facilitating the adventure process. In D. Prouty, J. Panicucci & R. Collinson (eds), *Adventure Education: Theory and Applications* (pp. 101–123). Champaign, IL: Human Kinetics.

Giddens, A. (1999). *Runaway World: How Globalization Is Reshaping Our Lives.* London: Profile.

Giddens, A. (1990). *The Consequences of Modernity.* Cambridge: Polity Press.

Giddens, A. (1991). *Modernity and Self-Identity: Self and Society in the Late Modern Age.* Cambridge: Polity Press.

Gill, T. (2010). *Nothing Ventured: Balancing Risks and Benefits in the Outdoors.* No city given: English Outdoor Council.

Giroux, H. (1988). *Teachers as Intellectuals: Toward a Critical Pedagogy of Learning.* South Hadley, MA: Bergin Garvey.

Grolnick, W.S., Ryan, R.M. & Deci, E.L. (1991). The inner resources for school achievement: Motivational mediators of children's perceptions of their parents. *Journal of Educational Psychology, 83*, 508–517.

Gruenewald, D. (2003). Foundations of place: A multidisciplinary framework for place-conscious education. *American Educational Research Journal, 40*(3), 619–654.

Gruenewald, D. & Smith, G. (eds). (2008). *Place-based Education in the Global Age*. New York: Lawrence Erlbaum Associates.

Henderson, B. (2010). Understanding heritage travel: Story, place, and technology. In S. Beames (ed.), *Understanding Educational Expeditions* (pp. 79–89). Rotterdam: Sense.

Hergenhahn, B. (1982). *An Introduction to Theories of Learning*. Englewood Cliffs, NJ: Prentice-Hall.

Hess, F.M. & Brigham, F.J. (2000). None of the above: The promise and peril of high-stakes testing. *American School Board Journal, 187*(1), 26–29.

Higgins, P. (2001). Learning outdoors: Encounters with complexity. In *Other Ways of Learning* (pp. 99–106). Marburg: European Institute for Outdoor Adventure Education and Experiential Learning.

Higgins, P. & Nicol, R. (2010). Professor Patrick Geddes (1854–1932): "Vivendo discimus"—by living we learn. In T.E. Smith & C.E. Knapp (eds), *Sourcebook of Experiential Education: Key Thinkers and Their Contributions* (pp. 32–40). London: Routledge.

Holyfield, L. (1999). Manufacturing adventure: The buying and selling of emotions. *Journal of Contemporary Ethnography, 28*(3), 3–32.

Holyfield, L., Jonas, L. & Zajicek, A. (2005). Adventure without risk is like Disneyland. In S. Lyng (ed.), *Edgework: The Sociology of Risk-taking* (pp. 173–186). New York: Routledge.

Hopkins, D. & Putnam, R. (1993). *Personal Growth through Adventure*. London: David Fulton.

Hovelynck, J. (2001). Beyond didactics: A reconnaissance of experiential learning. *Australian Journal of Outdoor Education, 6*(1), 4–12.

Hull, D. & Souders, J.C. (1996). The coming challenge: Are community colleges ready for the new wave of contextual learners? *Community College Journal, 67*(2), 15–17.

Hunt, J.S. (1990a). Philosophy of adventure education. In J.C. Miles & S. Priest (eds), *Adventure Education* (pp. 119–128). State College: Venture.

Hunt, J.S. (1990b). *Ethical Issues in Experiential Education* (2nd edn). Dubuque, IA: Kendall/Hunt.

Hunt, J.S. (1991). Ethics and experiential education as professional practice. *Journal of Experiential Education, 14*(2), 14–18.

Hursh, D.W. (2006). Marketing education: The rise of standardized testing, accountability, competition, and markets in public education. In E.W. Ross & R. Gibson (eds), *Neoliberalism and Education Reform* (pp. 15–34). Cresskill, NJ: Hampton Press.

Imel, S. (2000). *Contextual Learning in Adult Education*. Centre on Education, Training and Employment, Practice Application Brief no. 12. Columbus: OH: ERIC Clearinghouse on Adult, Career, and Vocational Education.

Irwin, D., Straker, J. & Hill, A. (2012). Educating outdoors in times of global crisis. In D. Irwin, J. Straker & A. Hill (eds), *Outdoor Education in Aotearoa New Zealand: A New Vision for the Twenty First Century* (pp. 12–25). Christchurch: CPIT.

Itin, C. (1999). Reasserting the philosophy of experiential education as a vehicle for change in the 21st century. *Journal of Experiential Education, 22*(2), 91–98.

Jess, M., Atencio, M. & Thorburn, M. (2011). Complexity theory: Supporting curriculum and pedagogy developments in Scottish physical education. *Sport, Education and Society, 16*(2), 179–199.

Joughin, G. (2010). The hidden curriculum revisited: A critical review of research into the influence of summative assessment on learning. *Assessment & Evaluation in Higher Education, 35*(3), 335–345.

Laing, J. & Crouch, G. (2009). Myth, adventure and fantasy at the frontier: Metaphors and imagery behind an extraordinary travel experience. *International Journal of Tourism Research, 11*, 127–141.

Leberman, S. & Martin, A. (2003). Does pushing comfort zones produce peak learning experiences? *Australian Journal of Outdoor Education, 7*(1), 10–19.

Legislation.gov.uk (n.d.). *Activity Centres (Young Persons' Safety) Act 1995.* Retrieved from http://www.legislation.gov.uk/ukpga/1995/15/contents.

Louv, R. (2008). *Last Child in the Woods: Saving Our Children from Nature-deficit Disorder.* New York: Algonquin Books.

Loynes, C. (1998). Adventure in a bun. *Journal of Experiential Education, 21*(1), 35–39.

Loynes, C. (2002). The generative paradigm. *Journal of Adventure Education and Outdoor Learning, 2*(2), 113–125.

Loynes, C. (2010). The British youth expedition: Cultural and historical perspectives. In S. Beames (ed.), *Understanding Educational Expeditions* (pp. 1–16). Rotterdam: Sense.

Loynes, C. (2013). Globalization, the market and outdoor adventure. In E. Pike & S. Beames (eds), *Outdoor Adventure and Social Theory* (pp. 135–146). London: Routledge.

Lupton, D. (2013). *Risk* (2nd edn). London: Routledge.

Lynch, P. & Moore, K. (2004). Adventures in paradox. *Australian Journal of Outdoor Education, 8*(2), 3–12.

Lyng, S. (1990). Edgework: A social psychological analysis of voluntary risk taking. *American Journal of Sociology, 95*(4), 851–886.

Macbeth, J. (2000). Utopian tourists: Cruising is not just about sailing. *Current Issues in Tourism, 3*(1), 20–34.

MacLeod, A.K., Williams, M.G. & Bekerian, D.A. (1991). Worry is reasonable: The role of explanations in pessimism about future personal events. *Journal of Abnormal Psychology, 100*, 478–486.

Mahoney, M.J. (1991). *Human Change Processes: The Scientific Foundations of Psychotherapy.* New York: Basic Books.

Mannion, G., Fenwick, A. & Lynch, J. (2013). Place-responsive pedagogy: Learning from teachers' experiences of excursions in nature. *Environmental Education Research, 19*(6), 792–809.

Martin, J. (2004). Self-regulated learning, social cognitive theory, and agency. *Educational Psychologist, 39*(2), 135–145.

Martinez, E. & Garcia, A. (2000). *What is "neo-liberalism?" A brief definition.* Retrieved from http://www.globalexchange.org/campaigns/econ101/neo liberalDefined.html

Mathis, W.J. (2003). No child left behind: Costs and benefits. *Phi Delta Kappan, 84*(9), 679–686.

117

Mathis, W. (2012). *Research-based Options for Education Policymaking*. Boulder, CO: National Education Policy Center. Retrieved from http://nepc.colorado. edu/files/pb-options-2-commcore-final.pdf

McInerney, D. & McInerney, V. (1998). *Educational Psychology: Constructing Learning* (2nd edn). Sydney, Australia: Prentice-Hall.

Melaville, A., Berg, A. & Blank, M. (2006). *Community-based Learning: Engaging Students for Success and Citizenship*. Washington, DC: Coalition for Community Schools.

Mercer, S. (2011). Understanding learner agency as a complex dynamic system. *System, 39*, 427–436.

Miles, J.C. & Priest, S. (eds). (1990). *Adventure Education*. State College, PA: Venture.

Miles, J.C. & Priest, S. (eds). (1999). *Adventure Programming*. State College, PA: Venture.

Milner, R. (2014). Scripted and narrowed curriculum reform in urban schools. *Urban Education, 49*(7), 743–749.

Morrison, K. (2008). Educational philosophy and the challenge of complexity theory. *Educational Philosophy and Theory, 40*(1), 19–34.

Mortlock, C. (1984). *The Adventure Alternative*. Milnthorpe: Cicerone Press.

Mullins, P. (2014a). A socio-environmental case for skill in outdoor adventure. *Journal of Experiential Education, 37*(2), 129–143.

Mullins, P. (2014b). Conceptualizing skill within a participatory ecological approach to outdoor adventure. *Journal of Experiential Education, 37*(4), 320–334.

Nakamura, J. & Csikszentmihalyi, M. (2002). The concept of flow. In C. Synder & S. Lopez (eds), *Handbook of Positive Psychology* (pp. 89–105). Oxford: Oxford University Press.

Nelsen, P. & Seaman, J. (2011). Deweyan tools for inquiry and the epistemological context of critical pedagogy. *Educational Studies: A Journal of the American Educational Studies Association, 47*(6), 561–582.

Nerlich, M. (1987). *Ideology of Adventure* (vols 1 & 2). Minneapolis, MN: University of Minneapolis.

Oxford Concise Dictionary (2nd edn). (2008). *Adventurous*. Oxford: Oxford University Press.

Oxford English Dictionary (n.d). *Adventure*. Retrieved from http://www.oed. com/view/Entry/2923

Oxford English Dictionary (n.d). *Challenge*. Retrieved from http://www.oed. com/view/Entry/30298

Oxford English Dictionary (n.d). *Mastery*. Retrieved from http://www.oed.com/ view/Entry/114791

Packer, M. (2001). The problem of transfer, and the sociocultural critique of schooling. *Journal of Learning Sciences, 10*(4), 493–514.

Palmberg, I.E. & Kuru, J. (2000). Outdoor activities as a basis for environmental responsibility. *Journal of Environmental Education, 31*(4), 32–36.

Passarelli, A., Hall, E. & Anderson, M. (2010). A strengths-based approach to outdoor and adventure education: Possibilities for personal growth. *Journal of Experiential Education, 33*(2), 120–135.

Piaget, J. (1977). *The Development of Thought* (A. Rosin, trans.). New York: Viking Press.

Piaget, J. (1980). *Adaptation and Intelligence* (G. Eames, trans.). Chicago, IL: University of Chicago Press.

Priest, S. (1999). The semantics of adventure programming. In J.C. Miles & S. Priest (eds), *Adventure Programming* (pp. 111–114). State College, PA: Venture.

Priest, S. & Gass, M.A. (1997). *Effective Leadership in Adventure Programming.* Champaign, IL: Human Kinetics.

Priest, S. & Gass, M.A. (2005). *Effective Leadership in Adventure Programming* (2nd edn). Champaign, IL: Human Kinetics.

Priest, S., Gass, M.A. & Gillis, L. (2000). *The Essential Elements of Facilitation.* Dubuque, IA: Kendall/Hunt. http://scholar.google.co.uk/citations?view_op=view_citation&hl=en&user=t8M2da EAAAAJ&citation_for_view=t8M2daEAAAAJ:d1gkVwhDpl0C

Reddy, S.G. (1996). Claims to expert knowledge and the subversion of democracy: The triumph of risk over uncertainty. *Economy and Society, 25*(2), 222–254.

Reeve, J. (2002). Self-determination theory applied to educational settings. In E.L. Deci & R.M. Ryan (eds), *Handbook of Self-determination Research* (pp. 183–203). Rochester, NY: University of Rochester Press.

Ritzer, G. (1993). *The McDonaldization of Society: An Investigation into the Changing Character of Contemporary Social Life.* London: Pine Forge Press.

Roberts, J. (2012). *Beyond Learning by Doing: Theoretical Currents in Experiential Education.* New York: Routledge.

Robinson, K. (2011). *Out of Our Minds: Learning to Be Creative.* Chichester: Capstone.

Roly Russell, A., Guerry, P., Gould, R., Basurto, X., Chan K., Klain, S., Levine, J. & Tam, J. (2013). Humans and nature: How knowing and experiencing nature affect well-being. *Annual Review of Environment and Resources, 38,* 473–502.

Ross, E.W. & Gibson, R. (2006). Introduction. In E.W. Ross and R. Gibson (eds), *Neoliberalism and Education Reform* (pp. 1–14). Cresskill, NJ: Hampton Press.

Ross, H., Higgins, P. & Nicol, R. (2007). Outdoor study of nature: Teachers' motivations and contexts. *Scottish Educational Review, 39*(2), 160–172.

Rubens, D. (1999). Effort or performance: Keys to motivated learners in the outdoors. *Horizons, 4,* 26–28.

Ryan, R. & Deci, E. (2000). Self-determination theory and the facilitation of intrinsic motivation, social development, and well-being. *American Psychologist, 55*(1), 68–78.

Schoel, J., Prouty, D. & Radcliffe, P. (1988). *Islands of Healing: A Guide to Adventure Based Counseling.* Hamilton, MA: Project Adventure.

Seaman, J. & Nelsen, P. (2011). An overburdened term: Dewey's concept of "Experience" as curriculum theory. *Education and Culture, 27*(1), 5–25.

Shields, C. (2012). *Transformative Leadership in Education: Equitable Change in an Uncertain and Complex World.* New York: Routledge.

Sibthorp, J., Paisley, K. & Gookin, J. (2007). Exploring participant development through adventure-based recreation programming: A model from the National Outdoor Leadership School. *Leisure Sciences, 29*(1), 1–18.

Sibthorp, J., Paisley, K., Gookin, J. & Furman, N. (2008). The pedagogic value of student autonomy in adventure education. *Journal of Experiential Education, 31*(2), 136–151.

Smith, G. (2002). Place-based education: Learning to be where we are. *Phi Delta Kappan, 83*(3), 584–594.

Smith, G. & Sobel, D. (2010). *Place and Community Based Education in Schools.* New York: Routledge.

Sobel, D. (2005). *Place-based Education: Connecting Classrooms and Communities.* Great Barrington, MA: Orion.

Stefanou, C., Perencevich, K., DiCintio, M. & Turner, J. (2004). Supporting autonomy in the classroom: Ways teachers encourage student decision making and ownership. *Educational Psychologist, 39*(2), 97–110.

Sternberg, R. (2000). Identifying and developing creative giftedness. *Roeper Review, 23*(2), 60–64.

Sternberg, R. (2003). *Wisdom, Intelligence, and Creativity Synthesized.* Cambridge: Cambridge University Press.

Stonehouse, P. (2010). Virtue ethics and expeditions. In S. Beames (ed.), *Understanding Educational Expeditions* (pp. 17–23). Rotterdam: Sense.

Stonehouse, P., Allison, P. & Carr, D. (2011). Aristotle, Plato, and Socrates: Ancient Greek perspectives on experiential learning. In T.E. Smith & C.E. Knapp (eds), *Sourcebook of Experiential Education: Key Thinkers and Their Contributions* (pp. 18–25). London: Routledge.

Sugarman, D.A., Doherty, K.L., Garvey, D.E. & Gass, M.A. (2000). *Reflective Learning: Theory and Practice.* Dubuque, IA: Kendall/Hunt.

Swarbrooke, J., Beard, C., Leckie, S. & Pomfret, G. (2003). *Adventure Tourism.* London: Routledge.

Tauritz, R.L. (2012). How to handle knowledge uncertainty: Learning and teaching in times of accelerating change. In A.E.J. Wals & P.B. Corcoran (eds), *Learning for Sustainability in Times of Accelerating Change.* Wageningen: Wageningen Academic Publishers.

Taylor, C. (1991). *The Ethics of Authenticity.* Cambridge, MA: Harvard University Press.

Tooth, R. & Renshaw, P. (2009). Reflections on pedagogy and place: A journey into learning for sustainability through environmental narrative and deep attentive reflection. *Australian Journal of Environmental Education, 25,* 95–104.

Varley, P. (2006). Confecting adventure and playing with meaning: The adventure commodification continuum. *Journal of Sport and Tourism, 11*(2), 173–194.

Varley, P. (2013). Rationalization and new realms of the commodity form. In E.J. Pike & S. Beames (eds), *Outdoor Adventure and Social Theory* (pp. 34–42). London: Routledge.

Vygotsky, L. (1978). *Mind in Society: The Development of Higher Psychological Processes.* Cambridge, MA: Harvard University Press.

Walle, A. (1997). Pursuing risk or insight: Marketing adventures. *Annals of Tourism Research, 24*(2), 265–282.

Walsh, V. & Golins, G. (1976). *The Exploration of the Outward Bound Process.* Denver, CO: Colorado Outward Bound School.

Wang, N. (1999). Re-thinking authenticity in tourism experiences. *Annals of Tourism Research, 26*(2), 349–370.

Ward, S. (2012). *Neoliberalism and the Global Restructuring of Knowledge and Education*. London: Routledge.

Wattchow, B. & Brown, M. (2011). *Pedagogy of Place: Outdoor Education for a Changing World*. Melbourne: Monash University Publishing.

Weaver, W. (1948). Science and complexity. *American Scientist, 36*, 536–544.

Weber, M. (1922/1968). *Economy and Society: An Outline of Interpretive Sociology*. G. Roth & C. Wittich (eds). Los Angeles, CA: University of California Press.

Whitehead, A.N. (1929). *The Aims of Education and Other Essays*. New York: Free Press.

Whitty, G. (2002). *Making Sense of Education Policy*. London: Sage.

Wikipedia. (n.d.). *Adventure*. Retrieved from http://en.wikipedia.org/wiki/Adventure.

Wolfe, B. & Samdahl, D. (2005). Challenging assumptions: Examining fundamental beliefs that shape challenge course programming and research. *Journal of Experiential Education, 28*(1), 25–43.

Wurdinger, S. (1997). *Philosophical Issues in Adventure Education* (3rd edn). Dubuque, IA: Kendall Hunt.

Wurdinger, S. & Potter, T. (eds) (1999). *Controversial Issues in Adventure Education*. Dubuque, IA: Kendall/Hunt.

Young, N., DaRosa, V.M.P. & Lapointe, J. (2011). On the origins of late modernity: Environmentalism and the construction of a critical global consciousness. *ANTROPOlógicas, 12*, 2–8.

Zink, R. & Leberman, S. (2001). Risking a debate—refining risk and risk management: A New Zealand case study. *Journal of Experiential Education, 24*(1), 50–57.

Zweig, P. (1974). *The Adventurer: The Fate of Adventure in the Western World*. Princeton, NJ: Princeton University Press.

Index

Page numbers in *italics* refer to figures.